Doris Dickey
Business Services

D1569516

The Health Care Manager's

GUIDE

TO

PERFORMANCE

APPRAISAL

Charles R. McConnell

Vice President for Employee Affairs
The Genesee Hospital
Rochester, New York

AN ASPEN PUBLICATION®
Aspen Publishers, Inc.
Gaithersburg, Maryland
1993

Library of Congress Cataloging-in-Publication Data

McConnell, Charles R.
The health care manager's guide to performance appraisal/
Charles R. McConnell
p. cm.

Includes bibliographical references and index.
ISBN 0-08342-0348-0
1. Medical personnel—Rating of. 2. Health facilities—Administration. I Title.
[DNLM: 1. Employee Performance Appraisal—methods. HF 5549.5.R3 M478h]
RA971.35.M279 1992
362.1'068'3—dc20
DNLM/DLC
for Library of Congress
92-17876
CIP

Copyright © 1993 by Aspen Publishers, Inc.
All rights reserved.

Aspen Publishers, Inc., grants permission for photocopying for limited personal or
internal use. This consent does not extend to other kinds of copying, such as copying
for general distribution, for advertising or promotional purposes, for creating new
collective works, or for resale. For information, address Aspen Publishers, Inc.,
Permissions Department, 200 Orchard Ridge Drive, Suite 200,
Gaithersburg, Maryland 20878

Editorial Resources: Barbara Priest

Library of Congress Catalog Card Number: 92-17876
ISBN: 0-8342-0348-0

Printed in the United States of America

1 2 3 4 5

Table of Contents

Preface

The Health Care Manager's Guide to Performance Appraisal is intended as a book of practical advice on all aspects of performance appraisal. Although the terminology of health care is employed and the examples are drawn from health care situations, and although health care sometimes presents appraisal problems not found in certain other situations, overall the book's topic rises above any particular industry setting. Wherever there is a need to be concerned about employee performance, wherever there are people working together in manager-employee relationships, wherever there are workers of any kind, with any skill or educational level, who look to others for feedback about their work, there is a need for fair and forthright appraisal of performance. In short, wherever people work at the direction of others there is a need for performance appraisal.

This book is meant to serve as a working performance appraisal guide for all managers who are called on to evaluate employee performance. It is also intended as a training resource for educating employees, evaluators and non-evaluators alike, on all aspects of appraisal. In addition, beyond dealing with the why and how of conducting effective appraisals this book is also meant to be a source of guidance in designing appraisal systems and modifying and updating existing systems.

The book is organized as follows:

Part I–Appraisal in Perspective establishes the primary objectives of performance appraisal, identifies the principal barriers to effective appraisal within the work organization, describes what must be done to avoid appraisal system failure, and develops the appraiser's outlook through consideration of the person who appraises employees as also the subject of appraisal by others.

Part II–The People Process: Doing Effective Appraisals is devoted to conducting performance appraisals within an organization's existing system. It includes preparing the appraiser and the employee, gathering information, actually writing an appraisal, observing schedules and other timing considerations, conducting the all-important appraisal interview, and utilizing the performance appraisal not as the end point of a period of employee behavior but as the beginning of a new period of employee performance.

Part III–The Mechanism: Designing an Integrated Appraisal System provides advice for the organization that might be considering complete overhaul of all or a significant part of its appraisal process or is perhaps considering the initial establishment of a formal appraisal program. This section addresses performance appraisal as the center of a larger management system of interrelated elements and suggests an orderly path from job analysis through job description and job specification and the establishment of objective measures of performance. Recognizing that the differing needs of specific organizations will dictate different paths for the establishment of fair and equitable systems, this section builds toward the establishment of a common desirable end: the requirements of an effective appraisal system.

Part IV–Other Appraisal Considerations is intended to deal with a number of dimensions of appraisal that may not concern all appraisers at all times but that are nevertheless important. Specifically addressed are:

- some of the traditional forms of appraisal that may still be applicable in limited circumstances
- the place of management by objectives, joint target setting, and other employee-involvement approaches in present day appraisal
- the unique problems presented by the appraisal of managerial personnel and professional employees
- the present-day legal implications of performance appraisal and how to minimize the likelihood of legal problems in appraising employees
- how to live with an inappropriate or inefficient appraisal system that the individual evaluator is unable to change

The what, why, and how of performance appraisal are addressed in considerable detail throughout the book. However, this is all presented in the hope that one critical message will come through the detail throughout: Over and above appraisal, the most important element in assessing performance is the relationship that exists between manager and employee. Regardless of the form, format, or structure of any particular appraisal system, if the relationship between manager and employee is all that it should be, then appraisal will be a mere formality, because both parties will know where they stand with each other at all times.

Rochester, New York
March, 1992

Part I
Appraisal in Perspective

1

Performance Appraisal: What and Why

THE PROCESS OF PERFORMANCE APPRAISAL: WHAT'S IN A NAME?

The label *performance appraisal* is both a name of convenience and an accurate description of the process discussed in these pages. This same process has been called, among other things, performance evaluation, performance assessment, performance review, employee evaluation, employee assessment, employee review, and even proficiency report and efficiency report.

The latter two labels, *proficiency report* and *efficiency report*, came from the names of the forms (and thus the designations of the systems) used by several government agencies. These designations are inappropriate; in appraising, one is doing much more than reporting, and neither proficiency nor efficiency properly describes the focus of the activity. Among the other labels the use of the word *review* also leaves much to be desired; in appraising, one is doing considerably more than reviewing.

Of the remaining designations for the process, all those beginning with the word *employee*, including the commonly used *employee evaluation* and *employee assessment*, are not appropriate labels for this activity. In each case the second word is accurate; *evaluation* and *assessment* rank high among the accepted synonyms for *appraisal*. It is the word *employee* that does not belong; it is not the employee—the person—who is evaluated. Rather it is the employee's performance that is evaluated.

Performance appraisal, performance evaluation, and *performance assessment* are all acceptable labels that reasonably describe the process they represent. It is, again, always performance that should be under scrutiny, and the manner of scrutiny should involve judgment of performance in a way that implies some degree of measurement. Appraisal, evaluation, and assessment all appropriately convey a sense of measurement; performance is not merely reviewed, although the process is still popularly referred to as a review in many quarters, and neither is it simply reported. Performance is appraised or evaluated; it is measured on some relative scale.

Some systems have reviewed, some have simply reported, some have genuinely appraised. Some systems (in fact, a majority of systems in use two or more decades ago) have focused on the person rather than the performance embodied in the person's actions.

For a number of reasons that will be explored in later pages, many appraisal systems in use today fall short of realizing their full potential. However, an apparent majority of today's appraisal approaches are solidly on the right track in being focused primarily on performance rather than on person; that is, they correctly presume to assess not what the person is but rather what the person does.

WHY APPRAISE PERFORMANCE?

One can count a number of organizational uses of performance appraisal as good reasons for appraising employee performance. These will be described later. Our question—why appraise performance?—is offered in the broadest, most fundamental sense possible, and the answer lies in the internal forces that cause people to behave as they do. The answer lies in human motivation.

Some managers seem to believe that employees should be motivated sufficiently by the rewards available in the organizational setting to change their behavior when problems are pointed out to them. These managers assume that wages and benefits and other material rewards are the primary goals that most employees work toward. However, it is a fallacy to assume that most organizational rewards encompass the major needs of people.

Fundamental Human Needs

In his well known need hierarchy, A. H. Maslow described the basic human needs as follows:[1]

- physiological needs—These are the most fundamental needs, those required to sustain life, such as food and shelter.
- safety needs—These include the need to feel reasonably free from harm from others and reasonably free from economic deprivation (in other words, job security).
- love needs—These include the needs to be liked by others and to be accepted into group membership, whether a work group, family group, or social group. These needs involve a sense of belonging.
- esteem needs—At this level in the hierarchy people experience the need for recognition, for approval, for the assurance that what one is doing is appreciated.

- self-actualization—According to Maslow, the need for self-actualization represents "a pressure toward unity of personality, toward spontaneous expressiveness—toward being creative, toward being good, and a lot else."

The Basic Needs of Employees

In an often cited survey conducted by the United States Chamber of Commerce, a sizeable number of first-line managers were asked to rank ten supposed morale factors in the order in which they believed these to be of importance to their employees.[2] That is, they were asked to rank these factors as motivating forces. In a second phase of the survey all employees of the same managers were asked to rank the same ten factors in order of importance to them as individual workers.

The managers guessed that the ten factors would appeal to their employees in the following order of importance:

1. good wages
2. job security
3. opportunity for promotion and growth
4. good working conditions
5. interesting work
6. organizational loyalty to employees
7. tactful disciplining
8. full appreciation of work done
9. understanding concerning personal problems and needs
10. being included on things

The employees placed the same morale factors in the following order of importance:

1. full appreciation of work done
2. being included on things
3. understanding concerning personal problems and needs
4. job security
5. good wages
6. interesting work
7. opportunity for promotion and growth
8. organizational loyalty to workers
9. good working conditions
10. tactful disciplining

The point of the foregoing pair of lists is of course to indicate that employees in general tend to place more emphasis on higher-order needs than on needs usually associated with purely materialistic factors. In desiring appreciation for work done employees seek to fulfill esteem needs; in wishing to be included on things and in desiring understanding concerning personal problems and needs employees seek to fulfill both esteem needs (participation as a fully included communicating partner) and love needs (the need to belong, to be accepted).

Maslow's need hierarchy has stood the test of nearly 50 years extremely well in providing insight into human behavior. However, it alone cannot explain why people may respond differently to different kinds of factors in the work situation. Another approach that has broadened general understanding of what moves people to perform is the motivation-hygiene theory of Frederick Herzberg.[3]

Motivators and Dissatisfiers: Needs and the Job

Rather than examining human needs and their fulfillment, Herzberg looked at the factors comprising and surrounding the job. He concluded that the true motivators lie in the work itself and that hygiene factors—those elements making up the environment that surrounds the work—are not motivators but are rather potential dissatisfiers. It follows that these potential dissatisfiers—wages, benefits, promotional opportunities, and such—must be reinforced periodically or they become actual dissatisfiers. That is, an annual pay increase may not do much to inspire more positive performance, but the *lack* of that increase may actively breed dissatisfaction and have an adverse effect on performance.

The true motivating factors, as Herzberg suggests, appear to include:

- the opportunity to learn and to achieve
- the opportunity to do work that is interesting, challenging, and meaningful
- the opportunity to assume responsibility and to become involved in determining how the work is done

The environmental factors exist in all aspects of the employee's relationship with the organization. If the environmental factors are all acceptable, they do not necessarily motivate. However, if they are *not* acceptable, they can lead to dissatisfaction.

The environmental factors may be arranged into five categories:[4]

1. Communication
   - appreciation of one's efforts, praise when it is due

- knowledge of the organization's activities and intentions, inclusion in the employer's goals and plans
- knowledge of where one stands with the organization at any given time
- confidentiality in personal dealings with management, tactful disciplining and reasonable privacy

2. Growth potential
   - the opportunity for advancement: career ladders, and promotional paths
   - encouragement to grow: skill training, tuition assistance, management training for potential supervisors

3. Personnel policies
   - reasonable accommodation of personal needs, as in work scheduling, vacation scheduling, sick time benefits
   - reasonable feeling of job security
   - organizational loyalty to employees
   - respect for one's origins, background, and beliefs
   - fair and consistent treatment relative to other employees

4. Salary administration
   - fair salary and benefits relative to others in the organization, in the community, and in one's specific occupation

5. Working conditions
   - actual physical working conditions relative to what is expected or desired

Addressing Needs through Performance Appraisal

No single aspect of management, no specific management tool or employee relations approach, can uniformly address all of the potential opportunities identified within the true motivating factors while also uniformly reinforcing all of the potential employee dissatisfiers. Indeed, accomplishing this is what the job of management—getting things done through people—is all about. Performance appraisal, however, can go a great distance in the proper direction.

Consider the ways in which performance appraisal, properly applied, can address both the motivators and the potential dissatisfiers:

- All of the motivators previously identified involve the satisfaction of human needs of the higher orders. As expressed, all of them also directly suggest employee development—the opportunity to grow as a performer and thus as a person. In making the beginnings of growth and development possible, performance appraisal is providing a service of lasting value to employee and organization alike. In brief, the motivators all involve aspects of employee development and performance appraisal enhances employee development.

- The environmental factors—the potential dissatisfiers—are addressed in varying degrees through performance appraisal. Foremost is the entire realm of employee communication, the fulfillment of human needs through praise, acknowledgment, appreciation, inclusion, information, and such. And although an appraisal system may itself have no power to affect the shape or form of certain environmental factors—for example, the appraisal system does not dictate the details of a salary administration system or the existence of certain personnel policies—the appraisal system provides a mechanism through which employees learn about the environmental factors and management learns how employees are reacting to those factors.

However, we appraise performance for reasons that are far more down-to-earth than the calculated satisfaction of people's needs. We appraise performance so that we may maintain or improve upon the results of employees' efforts, and so that we may benefit employees and the organization by increasing people's capabilities. Also, to be complete in assembling reasons for appraising performance, we need to appraise performance because of outside requirements placed upon us.

PERFORMANCE APPRAISAL'S PRIMARY OBJECTIVES

The primary objectives of performance appraisal may be summarized as follows:

1. to maintain or improve performance in the job the employee presently holds
2. to enhance the development of employees so as to:
   - provide the organization with persons capable of accepting greater responsibility
   - aid those employees who seek growth and advancement

In addition, for the individual employee the normal performance appraisal cycle should provide a clear picture of both status and prospects. That is, when this cycle's appraisal has been delivered and discussed the employee should know:

- how he or she has been seen as performing up to the present
- where he or she can expect to be heading within the coming months

Note that the first listed objective is to maintain or improve performance in the job the employee presently holds. There are many instances in which employee performance is completely satisfactory and little if any improvement is likely. However, it is critically important that the manager make every reasonable effort to ensure that this satisfactory performance remains satisfactory.

In short, performance appraisal should exist to maintain or improve performance and to enhance employee development.

ACCREDITATION AND REGULATION SPEAK UP

Based on the potential benefits of the fulfillment of its primary objectives, performance appraisal makes its own case for its importance as a management practice. However, performance appraisal has also become a necessity in health care for all organizations that are accredited by various agencies. For example, the Joint Commission on Accreditation of Healthcare Organizations (the Joint Commission) calls overall for: "A periodic performance evaluation for each employee, based on a job description, and for each person providing direct patient care or support services under a contract, who is not subject to a clinical privileging process."[5]

Specifically in regard to nursing departments, the Joint Commission requires that: "Documented evidence of licensure and current clinical competence in assigned patient care responsibilities is reviewed and approved by the hospital before these nursing personnel engage in patient care activities." This passage is followed immediately by: "The performance of these nursing personnel in the hospital is evaluated."[6]

In addition, the foregoing passages quoted from the Joint Commission Standards are described as "key factors in the accreditation decision process." This means that these are among the characteristics considered most important to the accreditation process and thus the characteristics most likely to result in unfavorable findings if found lacking.

Further, regarding what constitutes "periodic," the Joint Commission recommends an annual evaluation.

In addition to accrediting bodies, a number of states that periodically survey health care institutions for regulatory compliance also call for documented evidence of employee performance appraisal.

There are numerous references to performance appraisal in many of the laws that govern employment practices, not legally requiring appraisal, but rather implying its necessity and indicating how appraisals figure in actual and potential legal actions. Legislation has provided much of the pressure that has gone into changing the shape of performance appraisal. For example, it is presently clear, as will be elaborated on in Chapter 17, that an honest, well documented, objective appraisal can be an organization's best defense against a charge of unjust termination of employment.

PERFORMANCE APPRAISAL PAST, PRESENT, AND FUTURE*

Performance appraisal as we know it has undergone some significant changes since its beginnings. However, the change from the review or perhaps evaluation of 20 or 30 years ago to the appraisal of today occurred not all at once, but rather in occasional bursts of improvement throughout decades of otherwise imperceptible change.

The majority of appraisal approaches have included the use of evaluation forms on which judgments were entered against certain requirements. The requirements were typically found on a vertical scale; that is, they appeared in the form of a list ranging down the left hand side of a page. The judgments were typically applied on a horizontal scale; that is, by making marks along lines or by entering something in boxes or spaces arrayed beneath a number of headings appearing across the top of the page. In general the vertical scale provided the basis for each judgment and the horizontal scale provided the degree of success or the supposed value of the performance.

Phase I: Unsupported Judgment in Two Dimensions

The first phase in the evolution of performance appraisal lies largely in the past. If it persists at all, perhaps in a few isolated pockets of resistance, it probably should be rooted out and eliminated for good.

In this phase the vertical scale consisted largely of a listing of personality characteristics. Although such a scale might have asked for an assessment of quantity of work and even quality of work, it largely called upon the evaluator to assess the employee's cooperativeness, adaptability, dependability, and attitude, among other personality based factors, and perhaps even asked the rater to evaluate appearance as well. Unless an employee's job was such that output could be counted or otherwise actually measured, or if perhaps the particular system called upon the evaluator to comment on attendance, the system based an employee's entire rating on personality judgments rendered by an individual—the average supervisor or manager—who was totally unqualified to make such judgments.

An unqualified judgment of a personality factor on the vertical scale was usually compounded by a judgment call as to which heading or box on the horizontal scale best described the employee's degree of acceptability. The evaluator might have to choose from, for example, unsatisfactory, below standard, at standard, above standard, exceptional, and outstanding. Thus we are left with subjective assessment compounding subjective assessment, yet purporting to represent evaluation of performance.

---

*An earlier version of this section appeared in Charles R. McConnell, "In Search of Objective Measurement in Performance Appraisal," *The Health Care Supervisor*, vol. 10, no. 2 (December, 1991) pp. 69–77.

Phase II: Vertical Scale Meets Job Description

Performance appraisal systems have changed largely to the extent that most vertical scale problems have been fixed or are gradually being fixed. It is now widely recognized that the most rational source of factors against which an individual will be assessed is the individual's job description. Indeed, the faithful use of the job description as the basis for an employee's appraisal can remove most of the evaluation from the realm of personality assessment. There are still bound to be personality effects in many appraisals—after all, evaluators frequently hold different employees in differing levels of regard, and personal likes and dislikes will sometimes surface—but the change from legitimizing personality assessment to stressing job requirements has gone a long way toward establishing performance appraisal on a productive track.

Many organizations' appraisal systems are hung up in this second phase of appraisal. Assessment is based on job description requirements, but these requirements continue to be judged using five, six, or more subjective assessments that range across the horizontal scale from, essentially, "no good at all" to "perfect." With appraisal systems in this phase of evolution, subjective assessment is still required but no longer does it compound an unqualified assessment of personality.

Phase III: Refining the Vertical and Trimming the Horizontal

The third phase of performance appraisal, which is finding growing acceptance as appraisal becomes more deeply rooted in our management systems, involves further alterations of the vertical scale and dramatic change in the horizontal scale.

In regard to the vertical scale, job description steps or task descriptions are being replaced by two kinds of elements:

1. specific task steps for which output can be measured in absolute terms (for example, so many pieces, units, visits, or whatever)
2. discretely identified criteria that permit assessment of narrow areas of performance in simple terms (for example, something that can be said to have been done or not done, or reference to a so-called standard that can be said to have been not met, met, or exceeded)

Implied in the foregoing element descriptions are essential changes in the horizontal scale; that is, getting away from five or six (or, in some systems, as many as ten or a dozen) judgments of good, poor, or otherwise, and replacing these with fewer, more specific choices. More will be said later concerning the design of the choices on the horizontal scale relative to the job requirements spelled out on the vertical scale.

Performance appraisal as a management technique continues to evolve as appraisal systems are made more practical, more pertinent to the task of evaluation, more based on reasonably measurable criteria, and more legally defensible. However, regardless of the nature of the appraisal system of the day there will remain most of the issues, largely related to the value and validity of appraisal itself, that have divided organizations for years on the subject of appraisal.

EVALUATING PERFORMANCE APPRAISAL

Few management techniques garner as much criticism as performance appraisal. Certainly no process as widely applied as performance appraisal is subject to the amount of criticism levied at appraisal. Much of the criticism, however, arises from knowledge of evaluator discomfort and from apparent uses—and misuses—of appraisal results.

It has been stated that the primary objectives of performance appraisal are, first, performance improvement, and second, employee development. However, there are data demonstrating that these objectives are not always primary. A survey of more than 300 organizations revealed the following about the extent of use of the half-dozen most cited applications of appraisals:[7]

compensation decisions..75%
performance improvement 48%
feedback to employees...40%
documentation of performance 30%
promotion...25%
training (identifying needs)..7%

Arguments range hot and heavy over whether performance appraisal should be used for compensation decisions, yet one can see as many as three-fourths of organizations using it in just this way. We hear and read much affirmation of performance improvement as the number one objective of appraisal, yet only just less than half of organizations appear to use it for this purpose. And we see the notion of employee development showing up as the use of appraisals in promotion in perhaps one-fourth of organizations.

Appraisal itself gets a poor rating from many people involved in both sides of the process and likewise from much current literature. It is clear that there are some broadly conflicting perceptions of what constitutes true performance appraisal, and it is also clear that the theory and intent behind appraisal is rarely matched by performance appraisal in practice. There is a general perception that a great many existing appraisal systems fail to meet some or all of their stated objectives.

A poor view of appraisal also arises because of the kinds of issues that must often be dealt with. Whatever is dealt with in an individual appraisal, the primary objectives of the process must remain positive. Therefore, the person who appraises others is faced with the task of positively presenting information that may convey undeniable negative implications—that is, criticism remains criticism no matter how fairly it is expressed.

If no reasonable appraisal system exists, the manager's ability to monitor performance levels and to inspire change is impaired. An effective appraisal system can enhance employee morale, for example, but even a good system cannot guarantee a "good" corporation or a "good" place to work. However, a poor system can serve as a virtual guarantee of morale problems, increased costs, excess turnover, and increased disciplinary actions and legal actions.

Performance appraisal is often left essentially to run on its own, but simply having the system does not guarantee effectiveness.

Appraisal frequently gets bad press because it seems to encourage the comparison of employees with each other, often turning appraisal into a game in which employees compete for scores. Management has been learning, however, that the most valid comparisons of employee performance involve comparing the individual employee with himself or herself over time. It is clearly risky to compare one person with another, and clearly much more equitable to compare each with a common standard so that, over time, each may be compared to himself or herself instead of with others.

It is possible to overdo the formality of performance appraisal. Employees deserve and ordinarily want feedback on their performance, but they do not especially want more formal appraisal—they want more frequent and continuous informal appraisal (day-to-day or casual feedback).[8] When appraisal tends to be used in place of informal communication its image becomes more tarnished.

It must be remembered that most of any employee's performance is usually successful or at least marginally acceptable. Rarely is any particular employee a total loss in a job. Therefore, appraisal, rather than being viewed as critical or punitive, might be better viewed for its true capability—as a process that can show the employee how to do better. If done correctly, appraisal can communicate the organization's expectations to the employee and gauge how well the employee met those expectations. However, appraisal should also convey that employees are accountable for their performance and responsible for their own mistakes. Unfortunately, this latter message concerning accountability and responsibility is often seen as appraisal's primary message.

Finally, appraisal often gets a totally undeserved rap in being made to take the blame for other management failings. Performance is related to the total environment in which the employee works, and good management and effective leadership can and frequently do inspire good performance. When a technique is applied arbitrarily, inconsistently, or incorrectly, the technique itself is not to blame.

As a management technique performance appraisal takes sufficient criticism that its value in the organization might occasionally be questioned. However, it is probably fair to say that appraisal is here to stay, regardless of what criticism might be heaped on it. If this is the case, then the healthiest position to take regarding the organization's appraisal system is to learn the system inside out, help to improve it when needed, and apply it in good faith.

NOTES

1. A. H. Maslow, "A Theory of Human Motivation," *Psychological Review* 50 (1943): 370–96.

2. Chamber of Commerce of the United States, *Washington Review*, 1966.

3. F. Herzberg et al., *The Motivation to Work* (New York: John Wiley & Sons, Inc., 1969).

4. Charles R. McConnell, *Managing the Health Care Professional* (Gaithersburg, Maryland: Aspen Publishers, Inc., 1984) 86–87.

5. *Accreditation Manual for Hospitals (AMH), 1991*, Joint Commission on Accreditation of Healthcare Organizations, MA.1.5.5, Management and Administrative Services, p. 79.

6. *Ibid,* NC 2.4.1 and 2.4.1.1, Nursing Care, p. 134.

7. Alan H. Locher and Kenneth S. Teel, "Appraisal Trends," *Personnel Journal*, vol. 67, no. 9 (September 1988): 140.

8. Jim Laumeyer and Tim Beebe, "Employees and Their Appraisal," *Personnel Administrator*, vol. 33, no. 12 (December 1988): 76–77.

2

The Problem with Appraisal
Is Appraisal*

PERFORMANCE APPRAISAL: THE PROBLEM CHILD OF MANAGEMENT PROCESSES

The title of this chapter is deliberately misleading. The problem with appraisal is not appraisal itself; however, appraisal is frequently regarded as though it is indeed a problem process of questionable if not negative overall value.

It was suggested in the previous chapter that performance appraisal suffers from an unfavorable reputation in some quarters. A poor reputation that attaches to a specific appraisal system in a particular organization may be well deserved for any number of reasons that will be brought out in this chapter. However, appraisal itself has a somewhat tarnished image overall. This has probably come about because of the experiences of many people, appraised and appraisers alike, have had with weak, inadequate, or failing systems. Also, the negative image of performance appraisal has been fostered to a significant extent in periodical literature.

Performance appraisal is one of the topics most often written about in business literature, especially in the periodicals devoted to human resource management. It is relatively easy to find magazine and journal articles that focus at length on the perceived shortcomings of appraisal, sometimes even to the extent of using the questionable journalistic tools of sarcasm and ridicule. True, these negative treatments usually include a paragraph or two about "how to make it right"—except for those few that go so far as to suggest abandoning appraisal altogether—but a few positive generalizations do not reverse the negative message that has been sent.

Thus there are people in work organizations who, through legitimate experience, are not kindly disposed toward appraisal, and they receive reinforcement in their negativity from the literature they turn to for information and advice. However, no author dealing with performance appraisal has been been able to

*Portions of this chapter first appeared in Charles R. McConnell, "Bringing Performance Appraisal's Most Common Problems Into the Open," *The Health Care Supervisor,* vol. 10, no. 1 (September, 1991).

establish reasonably that appraisal has no legitimate place in business. Most negative treatments of appraisal are correct as far as they go; there are some common, undeniable problems that arise with appraisal again and again. The problems are fairly easy to see, but the solutions are not always apparent. The published critics of performance appraisal, however, prove only that with appraisal, as with many other circumstances, criticism is far easier than correction.

WHY APPRAISAL SYSTEMS FAIL

Most working managers do not have to be told there is a credibility gap concerning performance appraisal. That gap lies between the expectations held of performance appraisal and the reality of its results.

In the literature of performance appraisal, in the words of authors of packaged appraisal systems, and in the claims of consultants, we can find a great deal of promise as to what we should expect appraisal to accomplish for employees and for the organization. Much of this promise is never borne out. Frequently, the individual manager's view of performance appraisal suggests more problems than benefits, and what may have been sold with promise seems instead to have delivered, at best, annoyances, and at worst, obstacles.

The following paragraphs will identify, isolate, and examine the kinds of problems most likely to complicate or frustrate the operation of a system of performance appraisal or cause practical system failure. Each major problem area presents its own particular difficulties, and in practice each has been alternately addressed or avoided in a number of ways, with varying degrees of success. Regardless of past successes or failures, however, each problem area continually begs to be addressed in some positive fashion, since each can—and often does—destroy an appraisal system altogether or at least keep it from becoming what it could be.

The common problems of performance appraisal fall into the following groupings:

- motivational weaknesses and shortcomings
- confusion as to what is being evaluated
- system administration failings, including some that might be better described as implementation problems
- discomfort of evaluators
- fear of legal repercussions

MOTIVATIONAL PROBLEMS

One of the largest areas of difficulty with appraisal concerns managers' attitudes toward the process and their willingness to make it work.

A 1985 study of performance appraisal practices showed that specific appraisal forms or practices made little apparent difference in how well appraisal systems worked. Rather, the critical factors in determining how well appraisal worked were the actions taken by higher management to reinforce performance appraisal's importance.[1]

Fully successful performance appraisal requires total management support. However, many top management groups give performance appraisal lip service only; appraisal is something they require their lower level managers to do, but it is not something that top management itself does. Top management may verbally espouse performance appraisal but do so only because they view the process as a necessary evil, a requirement of regulatory or accreditation bodies, or simply because of superficial acceptance of appraisal as "something we should do."

How well an appraisal system works can be related directly to actions taken by management to reinforce the importance of appraisal. If top management's attitude is casual or seemingly unconcerned—"Appraisal? Great stuff. Make sure all of your managers appraise their people every year, okay?"—this will be transparent the instant the managers who are required to do the appraisals notice that there is no follow up after those few words. A casual attitude on the part of top management frequently results in a casual attitude on the part of supervisors and middle managers.

Performance appraisal will have no chance of realizing its full potential unless all concerned believe in the process and its value. Too many views of appraisal suggest it is indeed a necessary evil—we are doing this because it is required of us—and its implied converse—if this were not required, we probably would not be doing it. The top-down attitude toward appraisal is probably the strongest force in shaping managers' motivation regarding appraisal. And if the majority of supervisors and managers are not especially motivated to make appraisal work, appraisal is then addressed in some fairly commonly encountered ways:

- It automatically assumes a low priority position among the manager's tasks.
- It becomes a freely postponable activity, one that can always be slid to next week or next month as something "more important" arises.
- The smaller but nevertheless essential parts of the task, like collecting anecdotal notes and other input over time, do not get done.
- When appraisal is finally dealt with directly, it is usually given far less time than it deserves.

Lack of top management support is usually felt most strongly by the highest level in the structure that does *not* get evaluated. This might be, for example, the department head who gets no evaluation from his or her superior (administrator, assistant administrator, or whomever) but is expected to evaluate a number of subordinate managers and ensure that these managers in turn evaluate all of their employees. This department head is put in a position of having to adhere to a system that top management has, by its own behavior, ignored. In effect, the organization's top managers are saying, "Do as we say, not as we do."

Difficult Problems to Fix

Motivational problems are the most difficult performance appraisal problems to solve. It is easy to say that motivation comes from the top down; however, if the organization's top manager exhibits a lack of motivation concerning performance appraisal it is unlikely that any subordinate managers are going to change that. One can, of course, make an effort to convince the top manager of the value of actively supporting appraisal, but no subordinate manager can guarantee the top manager's participation and support.

If top management is not the primary source of performance appraisal motivation, it remains for the subordinate manager, whether department head, middle manager, or first-line supervisor, to become that source for his or her own department or group. This can be difficult because it must either stem from a sincere belief in appraisal or result from a determined self sales effort on the value and necessity of appraisal.

WHAT IS BEING EVALUATED?

The answer to this question ought to be obvious: it is performance that is evaluated. However, the focus of appraisal often strays from performance to personality.

In years past it was generally thought to be acceptable to evaluate aspects of personality. One need only examine a few appraisal forms from 15 or 20 years ago to appreciate that the majority of so-called evaluation criteria were aspects of personality or were strongly influenced by personality. Table 2–1 lists appraisal criteria taken from an actual, long-used appraisal system. As suggested by these so-called criteria, past appraisal systems routinely called for the evaluation of the employee for the likes of attitude, cooperativeness, dependability, and such. Not only do these criteria call for the assessment of personality characteristics, they also call for totally subjective judgments.

Some other formerly used criteria might be seen as less based in personality—for example, volume of work, quality of work, job knowledge, and effectiveness—and perhaps more measurable, but in most instances few objective

Table 2–1 Evaluation Criteria: Past Appraisal System

1. Quality of Work	7. Dependability
2. Volume of Work	8. Attitude
3. Effectiveness	9. Cooperativeness
4. Job Knowledge	10. Interpersonal Relations
5. Adaptability	11. Attendance
6. Initiative	12. Appearance

measures were available and evaluators fell back on subjective judgments influenced by personality. If the employee was seen as pleasant, cooperative, or a nice person, then as long as the few objective measures available were satisfied—if, for example, volume of work was considered sufficient—ratings on all criteria, objective or not, went in the same positive direction. Thus personality, not necessarily performance, was long the focus of performance appraisal.

Although personality-based criteria largely have given way to criteria based on job description requirements, there are still strong tendencies toward coloring performance assessments with personality judgments. Chances are that the person who is described as "sullen and grouchy" will not be rated as high as the employee who is "happy and friendly," although both may turn out identical quantity and quality of work.

The tendency to be lured into personality considerations essentially results in looking more at what the employee *is* than at what the employee *does*. This involves the evaluator's failure to differentiate between the results of an employee's behavior and the causes of that behavior.

Performance results from behavior, so it is appropriate to examine the results of behavior. However, it is inappropriate to attempt to infer causes for that behavior. For example, if you have an employee about whom you have had numerous visitor complaints of discourteous treatment, it is completely appropriate for you to cite these complaints in an evaluation as unacceptable behavior. However, it is not appropriate for you to describe the employee as rude, grouchy, or uncooperative. Doing so requires a giant step—one the supervisor is not qualified to make—from the fact of the behavior to the inference of cause.

Any appraisal system that depends on the evaluator to render personality judgments of employees is courting failure. At the very most such a system will be only a hollow annual exercise that the parties go through because it remains an organizational requirement. The overwhelming majority of managers are not qualified to render personality judgments, and even if they were qualified to do so the practice would be inappropriate because of the focus on the character of the performer and not the nature of the performance.

The focus of appraisal should always be on what the employee does, and never on what the employee is (or seems to be). At all times it should be performance that is evaluated, never personality. It is the results of the employee's behavior, and never the supposed causes of that behavior, that are legitimately appraised.

SYSTEM ADMINISTRATION BARRIERS

System administration problems are produced in part by some of the motivational problems previously discussed. Simply put, more people are conscientious about keeping performance appraisal alive and moving if they believe in the process. Also, because appraisals are often seen by managers as unpleasant and inordinately time consuming, they frequently tend to be pushed aside in favor of "more important" business.

Moving Right Along

Unless someone has central responsibility for moving evaluations through the system, some managers will run late with scheduled evaluations and some will do none at all. The average appraisal system, with the motivations that drive it being somewhat less than ideal, will grind to a halt of its own weight unless someone is there to remind evaluators of deadlines and generally to shepherd the process at every step. Without conscientious and timely system administration any performance appraisal system runs a high risk of failure.

System administration—or system maintenance, as it can also be called—is a must. Rarely, however, is there ever enough fully effective system administration. Unlike other kinds of systems in which there are frequent interfaces between people and computers or other machines, regardless of its degree of sophistication a performance appraisal system is largely human controlled. There is also room within the operation of the system for a significant amount of variability. For example, a simple computer system that provides spreadsheet capability will produce, within a limited range of variation, the same results for any of 20 people who might use it. But the average performance appraisal system can produce wide variations because each of 20 people who might use it has a significant amount of individual control.

System administration is elementary, but it has to be someone's priority. That task and priority usually reside in the human resource department. Depending on the particular system, it will be the job of the human resource department to:

- notify managers of evaluations due
- supply forms and instructions as necessary
- promptly follow up on delinquent appraisals

- ensure that other appropriate actions are initiated (for example, there will be payroll system implications if the system includes appraisal-based merit raises)
- file completed appraisals in personnel files

Training and Reinforcement

Except perhaps for the occasion of launching a completely new system, rarely is there enough training in how to apply the system appropriately. Too often training is overlooked beyond the initial classes in how to use the system. However, a performance appraisal system has special training needs.

Since an appraisal system is usually widely used—an organization using a single appraisal system, which is usually the case, can have thousands of employees rated by hundreds of evaluators—and because appraisal is subject to much human variation, it is necessary to strive for consistency of application. This suggests that evaluators need to be trained and periodically retrained in how to apply the system.

Performance appraisal training should ideally be accomplished with class-size groups of evaluators; bringing managers together in sufficient numbers will ensure that a maximum practical number of evaluators are exposed to the same advice in the same form at the same time. Variations in rating from manager to manager present a major problem with appraisal, so training in how to use the appraisal system must be totally consistent from manager to manager and group to group. Also, training must be reinforced periodically to reduce the risk of too much variation in ratings creeping into the system over time. While insufficient training may not itself cause an appraisal system to fail outright, it will contribute to glaring inconsistencies that can severely undermine the value of the system.

Implementation Inconsistencies: Unavoidable—But Controllable

The major problem mentioned above, variations in the application of the system from manager to manager, is a reality in most appraisal systems. Although this condition can be held to tolerable levels with regular refresher training, it will never be completely eliminated. When a large number of evaluators are interpreting and applying the same evaluation criteria, there are bound to be noticeable differences in results.

Some organizations have found this rating variation problem to be sufficiently significant to justify artificial "leveling" of ratings. A simple approach to rating leveling consists of determining the average of each evaluator's ratings, equating these averages across the organization, and scaling the evaluator's ratings proportionately above and below the average. On the positive side, this approach wipes out broad differences stemming from some evaluators' tendencies to be easy raters or strict raters. On the negative side, leveling evaluators' ratings to a common average discounts the real possibility that a particular work group may contain a preponderance of poorer or better performers than other groups. In other words, leveling takes out legitimate variations as well as variations based solely on interpretation and style.

Rating variations become an even greater problem in systems in which merit pay is dispensed according to evaluation score. A department manager who consistently scores higher than others is obtaining a larger share of the organization's merit money for the department. One way this can be corrected is to allocate a specific merit amount to each department according to the size of its personnel budget. For example, if the laboratory department's personnel budget is 8.2 percent of the total hospital budget, then the laboratory is allocated 8.2 percent of the available merit money. However, as in the use of score leveling, this process assumes that performance is evenly distributed across all departments.

Rating variations among managers sometimes have a particularly noticeable effect on employees who transfer. An employee may transfer from the department of a tough rater to that of a soft rater, or vice versa, and in the process may see his or her evaluation score change dramatically. Employees whose scores go up will not ordinarily be disturbed by this, but those whose scores go down may complain. Of course, not all of the drop in a score may be attributable to a stricter evaluator; some of the difference could be caused by the employee's still-expanding familiarity with the new job, but a significant decline in evaluation score may cause the employee to question or challenge the rating. Once again, regularly reinforced training is required to moderate the rating differences from manager to manager.

The often cited *halo effect*, though now not nearly as much of a problem as it was when appraisals were based entirely on personality, still presents some difficulties. This effect occurs when the evaluator allows the assessment of one or a few criteria, whether favorable or unfavorable, to influence his or her assessment on other criteria. That is, a good rating on an important criterion tends to elevate the ratings of other criteria; likewise, a poor rating tends to lower the ratings of other criteria.

As more appraisal systems have become job-description or criteria based, the halo effect has become less of a problem. It is easier to consider discretely different job-based rating criteria separately than it is to separate personality-based criteria for individual consideration. However, the need to consider all criteria independently of each other must be stressed in performance appraisal training.

DISCOMFORT OF EVALUATORS

Most people dislike having to give even honest, accurate, and timely feedback to others if this feedback is aimed primarily at correcting even minor shortcomings or weaknesses.[2] Research suggests that there is substantial evidence indicating that people do try to avoid transmitting unpleasant messages to each other.[3] Simply put, a great many people are hesitant to criticize others.

A significant proportion of evaluators experience some degree of discomfort with making judgments that potentially could affect people's income levels and career progress. The evaluating manager may be all too aware that a negative reflection on an appraisal could prevent an employee from obtaining a transfer to a more desired position. And if merit pay is linked with appraisal score, the manager is likewise aware that a lower score brings the employee a smaller pay raise. This discomfort is often alleviated—or perhaps it would be more appropriate to say that the discomfort is avoided—by making sure that all evaluations are positive, or at least not overtly negative. Therefore, the manager may subvert his or her true feelings about an employee's substandard performance and write a no-fault evaluation.

There seems to be a number of sometimes complex emotional barriers to the dispensing of unfavorable evaluation commentary. At times it appears that a great many managers simply do not like to provide any commentary that can be construed as criticism, especially knowing that it will have to be discussed with the employee face to face.

Invariably the manager who hesitates to "tell it like it is" is usually magnifying the true problems simply by thinking about them, dreading imagined confrontations that usually would have turned out not nearly as bad as imagined. The manager who collides with personal emotional barriers will often compensate by giving the employee a higher rating than deserved, distorting ratings and generally avoiding all negative commentary. And the manager who collides with emotional barriers will sometimes avoid even these no-fault approaches and procrastinate on the evaluation until forced by the system to hand in something. This circumstance reinforces the need for conscientious system administration; without the further discomfort of external pressure, the procrastinating manager may well never get around to the evaluation.

Since a given manager by nature may try to avoid sending unpleasant messages but still may appreciate the importance of the annual appraisal, it sometimes occurs that a number of smaller gripes accrue over the year; that is, criticism was not delivered when deserved, and a year's worth of negative material exists. One of two approaches is likely when the annual appraisal becomes a must: (1) the manager gets no braver simply because it is time for the required review, problems get glossed over, and the employee does not get an honest or helpful appraisal; or (2) the manager swallows his or her fears, opts for honesty, and the employee is hit with a "gotcha!" review. The honesty is certainly a step in the right direction, but surprise negatives are inappropriate.

Much of the difficulty experienced in trying to provide assertive, constructive, specific criticism is related to lack of appraisal skill, lack of understanding of the appraisal system, and lack of self confidence. However, if the first two of these are conscientiously addressed through periodic education, the manager's confidence level usually will improve sufficiently to enable a reasonable approach to appraisal.

The manager whose self confidence is shaky seems to approach appraisal thinking, "Who am I to be saying that this person is or isn't doing well on the job? That he (or she) has to change? Am I really qualified to do this?" And beyond this form of self questioning we occasionally find the blame-shouldering manager who embarks upon a guilt trip wondering, "Did I do everything I could possibly do to enable these employees to succeed? If they fail to perform as expected, isn't this my fault for not preparing them well enough?" Interestingly enough, the managers who experience this form of guilt are usually the managers who did everything possible to help the employees succeed; the managers who inadequately prepare their employees rarely entertain such thoughts.

Emotional barriers to doing appraisals will remain, but they can be minimized and controlled with higher management support and plenty of reinforcement. Barriers can also be mitigated by putting more care and planning into evaluation. For example, if you have thought far enough ahead to keep a running record of specifics to support an evaluation, you will have little trouble writing some fairly specific remarks that you can then support with the record if need be. But if you cannot be specific because you kept no details, you must then resort to more general comments, and you know that, if challenged, you cannot support a general comment, so again you experience another pressure toward glossing over a problem with an undeservedly high rating.

Granted, it takes a measure of courage to criticize another person. Recognizing this much, some evaluators "bite the bullet" and, believing that this is *the* time they must level with employees, turn each appraisal interview into what could be described at best as a pep talk and at worst as a chewing out. The courage to deal honestly must rather be tempered with the compassion of one caring person for another; the manager must exhibit the courage to do what needs doing and the compassion to do it with every human consideration.

FEAR OF LEGAL REPERCUSSIONS

One highly prevalent appraisal problem today centers about the fear of action, legal and otherwise, on the part of employees. The lesser concern involves internal action—complaints to management, grievances, or appeals through an internal system—by employees who are dissatisfied with their evaluation scores or with the contents of their appraisals otherwise. When there are unpleasant surprises in appraisals, when there are comments employees resent, or when scores are felt to be too low, some employees will complain. The knowledge that this happens is enough to keep some managers from being brutally honest. One admittedly easy rater described his tendency as "present avoidance of future grief."

There is less to fear concerning employee complaints when all aspects of an appraisal can be backed up with specifics. In this respect the shift from the assessment of personality to the assessment of performance has been a great help. Personality assessments are usually general and necessarily judgmental; they cannot be backed up with specifics or facts. However, performance assessments, properly rendered according to specific criteria and definable measures, greatly reduce the likelihood of unsupportable judgments entering into the process. It is the unsupportable judgments that cause trouble; as long as an assessment cannot be reasonably verified, it can be successfully protested or at least thrown into doubt.

The ability to attack productively that which cannot be proved is also behind many evaluators' fear of outside intervention from regulatory agencies, advocacy groups, and employees' attorneys. This fear has been intensified by the great deal of attention that the legalities of performance appraisal have received in recent literature. And much of this attention is justified; a great many employment-related legal actions, administrative proceedings as well as lawsuits, involve close scrutiny of employee appraisals. The inevitability of this kind of scrutiny suggests that appraisals need to be honest, straightforward, and as specific as possible, and especially that they be as verifiable as possible.

Consider the employee who comes under criticism for "carelessness, negligence, and general incompetence" and is fired. Perhaps, in the manager's mind, the employee was always this bad, and the manager finally ran out of patience. However, a complaint investigator or an attorney examines the employee's file and finds no previous indication of trouble, but rather finds three or four "satisfactory" appraisals. It is of just such circumstances that many of today's claims of unjust dismissal are made.

The best overall advice for avoiding legal trouble with appraisals is the same advice offered to managers who write up disciplinary actions and to persons who respond to employment reference requests: enter *nothing* that cannot be verified objectively. In other words, use no general statements and no subjective judgments. For example, do not describe the chronically tardy employee as "undependable" or even "always late;" rather, indicate that "chronic tardiness has been a problem," making sure that the employee's file includes the appropriate warnings listing the specific instances of tardiness.

A thorough discussion of performance appraisal relative to employment law appears in Chapter 17.

AN INESCAPABLE REQUIREMENT

The inescapable requirement of all who make performance appraisals is judgment. The trouble with personality-based appraisal is that it requires far too much judgment, most of it unsupportable. Modern job-description-based and criteria-based appraisal brings into play specific job-related factors and more objective measures than were previously available; in this fashion modern appraisal reduces the range within which judgment must be applied. Also, describing the performance of a job in a number of dimensions enables the evaluator to build an appraisal out of a larger number of fairly specific judgments rather than from just a few broader judgments. This has a tempering effect on most evaluators' judgments.

In the past there were significant judgment problems on both major axes of an appraisal: the vertical scale, which consisted of the listing of evaluation criteria (personality characteristics, etc.), and the horizontal scale, which consisted of a number of performance gradations (ranging, for example, from poor to excellent). Getting away from personality characteristics and going to specific evaluation criteria sufficiently narrowed the band of judgment on the vertical scale; it involves far less judgment to assess one aspect of task performance than once was required to assess, for example, "flexibility."

In many systems, however, degrees of unsupported judgment are still necessary on the horizontal scale. For example, one particular system still uses the following degrees of performance: unsatisfactory, usually at standard, standard, above standard, well above standard, and exceptional. One can raise dozens of questions about these so-called ratings: How far above standard is well above?; When does well above standard become exceptional?; What constitutes usually at standard?; and so on. Most of these terms defy precise definition, so almost every rating can be disputed.

The problems of the horizontal scale are being addressed gradually in newer systems that reduce the number of performance descriptors from six or more to no more than three and apply these fewer descriptors using standards of performance. Then, for any performance criterion to which a standard can be applied, instead of using unsatisfactory, exceptional, etc., one can limit the judgment of performance to standard not met, standard met, or standard exceeded.

More work is constantly being done in the development of objective measures and standards of performance, but not everything about any given job can be completely quantified or measured in absolute terms. Those who seek an appraisal system that eliminates all judgment on the part of the evaluator are bound for disappointment. The need for managerial judgment will remain prominent in performance appraisal; the challenge faced in developing today's systems is to ensure that the necessary managerial judgment is informed, rational, and supportable, and is applied consistently within a common framework by all who use the same system.

BEYOND APPRAISAL

The most commonly experienced problems of performance appraisal are capable of undermining an organization's appraisal process to the extent of giving some users excuses for not making the process work. (My boss doesn't evaluate me, so why should I bother to evaluate my employees? So what if I'm weeks late doing appraisals—nobody follows up on them, anyway.) Most appraisal systems exhibit some of the problems discussed in this chapter, so most systems carry baggage that makes them potentially less effective than they could be.

Whether performance appraisal truly works in a given group depends completely on the manager. Despite system shortcomings, if the manager remains on top of appraisal, treats it as an essential process, believes in performance appraisal, and genuinely tries to make the most of the process, appraisal will be a generally positive process within that group.

In the last analysis performance appraisal cannot be considered in a vacuum; it is not a process standing alone that a manager can turn on or off without affecting numerous other aspects of the supervisor-employee relationship. How the manager approaches the performance appraisal process sends the employee a clear message about the manager's measure of respect and concern for each employee. The manager who makes appraisals on time and who applies the process honestly, openly, and constructively thus sends the desired message to each employee. What, then, is likely to be the message inferred from the behavior of the manager whose staff appraisals are shallow, punitive, chronically late, or nonexistent?

NOTES

1. Mo Cayer, Dominic J. DiMattia, and Janis Wingrove, "Conquering Evaluation Fear," *Personnel Administrator*, vol. 33, no. 6 (June 1988) p. 97.

2. *Ibid.*

3. C. D. Fisher, "Transmission of Positive and Negative Feedback to Subordinates," *Journal of Applied Psychology,* vol. 64, no. 5 (1979) pp. 533–40.

3
The Appraiser's View: Improvement from the Bottom Up*

LOOK UPWARD TO RELATE DOWNWARD MORE EFFECTIVELY

As anyone who has risen from the ranks into management can attest, there are many significant differences between working as a manager and working as a nonmanagerial employee. Even though managers and nonmanagers must do a great many things differently from each other, the requirements placed upon them are identical in four important respects:

1. Managers and nonmanagers alike are subject to the same organizational goals and policies.
2. Nonmanagers and managers alike must be intimately familiar with the tasks of the department. (Nonmanagers will of course perform these tasks regularly while managers, perhaps performing them at times, must understand, teach, and judge task performance).
3. Managers and nonmanagers are subject to the delegation of tasks by their immediate superiors, as are all employees at all organizational levels except the very top.
4. Managers as well as nonmanagers are subject to performance appraisal by their immediate superiors.

Just as it is possible for managers to improve the effectiveness with which they delegate to employees by examining their delegating relationships with higher management, it is also possible for managers to become better evaluators of employee performance by examining and improving upon their performance appraisal relationships with higher management.

Most instruction and advice given to managers about performance appraisal is presented with a downward perspective; that is, it focuses only on the relationship between evaluator and subordinate. However, the manager can

*An earlier version of this chapter first appeared as Charles R. McConnell, "Improving Performance Appraisal From the Bottom Up," *The Health Care Supervisor*, vol. 8, no. 2 (January, 1991).

become a better evaluator of employees by working to improve his or her own appraisal relationship with higher management. Whether the individual manager's appraisal by higher management can be improved substantially by this process depends entirely on the attitude and receptivity of higher management. However, regardless of the manager's success in improving his or her own appraisal, the insight gained in the process will make the manager a better evaluator of employees.

SIMILAR NEEDS

The first-line supervisor or manager is simply another employee of the organization who happens to be one level removed from the rank and file. Even the so-called middle manager may be just one additional level removed from the rank and file. As rank-and-file employees are subject to the requirements of the manager, so too is the manager subject to the requirements of the next highest level of management.

As employees of the organization, the manager and the nonmanager bring similar, perhaps even largely identical, needs to work with them. It has been generally accepted for many years that we are motivated largely by our desire to fulfill the needs that drive us. For example, by seeking and maintaining an income we are acquiring the means to fulfill basic physiological needs; by obtaining approval and acceptance as a member of a group we are fulfilling certain sociological needs; by seeking job satisfaction and approval of what we do we are fulfilling certain psychological needs.

Although the mix of needs varies from one person to another, as separate groups nonmanagers and managers are not all that different from each other in terms of needs. That is, although the mix varies from person to person, the kinds of needs that motivate rank-and-file employees are generally the same kinds of needs that motivate managers. Therefore, if you carefully consider what you wish to obtain from your own performance appraisal, you can gain considerable insight into what most of your employees wish to learn from their appraisals.

Although there are secondary objectives concerned with employee development, the primary objective of performance appraisal is to maintain or improve performance in the job the employee presently holds. That is the organization's primary objective in using performance appraisal, and it is the objective you should have in mind when evaluating a subordinate. However, it is the manner in which you pursue the objective that makes the difference. The objective should be pursued in a way that, as completely as possible, gives the employee what he or she needs to obtain from the process. Consider some of the information and results that you, and therefore most of your employees, wish to carry away from the appraisal interview:

- a sense of having been dealt with fairly
- appreciation of your contribution to the organization

- recognition of special effort or exceptional accomplishments
- an indication of how your performance can be improved, and specific direction that will help you achieve improvement
- an honest assessment of your future prospects
- a sense of having been fairly rewarded materially (primarily in terms of pay increases) relative to others who are similarly situated
- the feeling that you have been allowed to contribute constructively to your appraisal discussion, and that you have been listened to and taken seriously.

The foregoing list may seem to represent a tall order, but it is not overly idealistic in terms of the desires, perhaps largely unarticulated, that most working people carry into their performance appraisal discussions. Examine these several points in two ways. First, are these points being satisfied for you in your own performance appraisal? If not, there are steps you can take that may help to improve your own appraisal. Second, are you doing the best you can to fill these needs for each employee you evaluate? If not, you can begin now by adopting these factors as guidelines for evaluating your employees.

Having thus increased your awareness of what both you and your employees wish to obtain from the appraisal process, you can then proceed to examine the manner in which your manager evaluates you and determine whether you can inspire any constructive change.

APPRAISAL TIMING

Most employees, managers included, are keenly aware of their scheduled evaluation dates. Does your own appraisal always occur on time? If yes, you fare better than many others in this respect. It remains only for you to apply this strict adherence to scheduled timing to your employees' evaluations. But if your own appraisal rarely occurs on time, see if you can do something to correct this practice.

Since performance appraisal is far from being the most comforting activity for most managers, there is a tendency for many managers to run late with appraisals. This condition is aggravated if the organization's performance appraisal system is not conscientiously administered. Some central function, ordinarily the human resource department, is usually responsible for keeping the system moving, for distributing forms, sending out reminders of due dates, and following up on delinquent appraisals. If system administration is lax, many managers tend to run even later with appraisals.

If your performance appraisal is chronically late, try reminding your manager shortly before the next one is scheduled. Most managers will take no offense at a reminder along the lines of: "I see my evaluation date is just two weeks away. Is there anything you would like me to do in the way of preparation?" Or, noting that your evaluation date is coming up you might innocently ask your manager if your appraisal interview has been scheduled yet so you can get it on your calendar. Such diplomatic reminders will not offend most managers, and a manager who might not yet have thought of your appraisal or who had simply assumed that you were giving it no particular thought might respond positively. You will then have your appraisal on time (or at least have it earlier than might otherwise be the case).

Regardless of your degree of success in improving the timing of your own appraisal, however, do not forget that timing means as much to most of your employees as it does to you. And if you have tended to run late with employee appraisals in the past, do not be offended if employees give you subtle reminders of upcoming review dates; they are probably using the same techniques with you that you are using with your manager.

CONSIDER SELF-APPRAISAL

If you enjoy a reasonable working relationship with your manager, and if you are not uncomfortable in doing so, offer to do a complete appraisal of your own performance using the same forms and criteria the manager will use. If you get to perform a self-appraisal, make sure that it is unbiased from either direction; that is, you should not see your manager's appraisal of you until after you have done your own, and your manager should not see your self-appraisal until after he or she has written your evaluation.

Should your manager be one who tends to forget appraisal interviews altogether, your self-appraisal will help ensure that a performance discussion does indeed occur. However, a self-appraisal's major benefits arise from an examination of the differences between your appraisal of yourself and your manager's evaluation of you. Consider, for example, that you are evaluated on twelve different job criteria. If the manager's evaluation and your self-appraisal are reasonably close together in the assessment of nine or ten of the twelve criteria, then you know immediately that your discussion of performance will be focused most constructively on the remaining two or three criteria on which you are not in agreement.

You may want to consider the use of self-appraisal by your employees, especially if you supervise primarily technical or professional workers. However, it is suggested that self-appraisal be presented as strictly optional, with absolutely no pressure perceived by employees who do not wish to participate. Many employees, uncomfortable with performance appraisal to begin with, are easily threatened by mandated self-appraisal. An employee who is so threatened will be trying so hard to second guess you that a useful self-appraisal will not be possible. Self-appraisal will be dealt with further in Chapters 7 and 16.

MAKING SURE THE INTERVIEW OCCURS

It is not unusual for the occasional manager to hand a completed appraisal to an employee while saying something on the order of: "Here's your evaluation; we'll talk about this sometime soon," or even: "Here's your evaluation; see me if you have any questions." The appraisal handed to the employee under such circumstances is ordinarily a no-fault review; that is, overall it will be favorable, if somewhat nonspecific, and anything it contains that might be described as criticism will be buried in vague terminology.

Should you receive a completed performance appraisal form under the circumstances just described, simply by handing it to you your manager has given you an open invitation to request an appraisal interview if one is not scheduled for you soon. The no-fault review, the kind that says generally you are doing a fine job without providing any particular detail, serves a single purpose—it gets your manager off the hook for another year as far as your appraisal is concerned.

Take steps to ensure that your appraisal interview happens. Make a direct request of your superior to talk about your appraisal. It is the rare manager who will deny—or find a creative way to avoid—such a direct request from an employee.

In dealing with your employees, you should of course schedule timely appraisal conferences. Do not make it necessary for them to prompt you in the manner just suggested for you to prompt your own delinquent manager. Remember that any behavior that stymies and frustrates you when encountered in your manager will also stymie and frustrate your employees when they encounter it in you. Do your conscientious best to avoid passing along inappropriate behavior.

Once you have been granted an appraisal interview, whether scheduled for you automatically or at your urging, take whatever steps you need to take to get the most out of it.

WORKING FOR A CONSTRUCTIVE INTERVIEW

If you do nothing to make it into something else, the appraisal interview by the manager who wants to get off the hook for another year will consist of little more than general compliments and complimentary generalities. Although a few minutes worth of nonspecific praise may be much easier for you to take than a few minutes worth of criticism, a goody-goody nonspecific appraisal will do nothing for you in your growth as a manager or health professional. Neither will goody-goody nonspecific reviews do anything constructive for your employees.

Go Armed with Questions

Prepare several questions—at least three or four—to take with you to your appraisal interview. Do not ask questions like "How do you think I'm doing?" Rather, prepare some pointed questions that deal with specific aspects of your performance, especially questions that stem from tasks and task elements covered in your job description. For example, in an effort to determine what your boss thinks about the way you are fulfilling your staff education responsibilities, you might want to ask something like, "What did you think of the departmental safety program I conducted during the last quarter? Do you think I could make it more compact without reducing its effectiveness?"

If your manager is conscientiously attempting to give you an honest and realistic appraisal, you may not have to use your prepared questions at all unless they deal with topics that you genuinely want to discuss over and above the points your manager raises. Your advance questions exist mainly in case your manager is inclined to fill the interview time with harmless generalities and friendly chit chat. If your manager is clearly trying to avoid the hard part—which is also the constructive part—of the interview, you will need your questions to get the discussion focused along constructive lines.

Challenge General Statements

It was British author G. K. Chesterton who said, "All generalizations are dangerous, including this one." Do not automatically accept generalizations about your performance, even highly complimentary ones. Challenge them.

Be especially wary of statements that hinge upon the words "always" and "never," as in "You always do this" or "You never do that." Rarely if ever are such statements completely true.

If, for example, your manager says to you, "Your group's productivity looks fine," you can then ask questions about whether productivity was better in some respects than others and where the differences lie, whether you appear to have maintained adequate productivity over the peak vacation period, whether it was evident in productivity during the last quarter that you had one employee on medical leave, and so on.

Almost every general statement your manager might make can be particularized by a series of specific, constructive questions from you.

Keep in mind that your objective during the appraisal interview should be to get your manager to talk about specific aspects of your performance. You do exactly that when you pose specific questions. Many managers, especially those who tend to think out loud better than they think on paper, will deliver a far more constructive appraisal when they can simply converse with you about the specifics of your performance.

You should expect, however, that as you challenge positive general statements you run the risk of drawing out some negative commentary. Perhaps your manager is indeed largely pleased with the way you are performing overall, but as you focus the discussion point by point and deal in turn with increasingly narrow aspects of your performance, the chances that negatives will emerge increase dramatically. Be prepared to accept the negatives—after all, if you are serious about real performance appraisal you will want to hear the honest negatives—and be prepared to ask how the negatives can be turned into positives in the future.

Request Corrective Guidance

Any specific criticism of your performance should be accompanied by constructive guidance on how you can go about improving that aspect of your performance. No criticism is constructive unless it includes the means for effecting correction, and criticism that is not constructive is not valid.

When your performance is criticized during your appraisal interview:

- If the criticism is general, ask for specifics. For example, if your manager says, "You've been a little sloppy in controlling overtime," ask for your boss's perception of how much you are off, what time period it applies to, and what he or she believes the cause might be.
- Ask for specific guidance, as in, "Okay, exactly what can I do, in addition to what I've already been doing, to help hold overtime down?"
- Secure a specific target. Whether suggested by you or your manager, but certainly discussed between you, your target for improvement should ideally be one on which you both agree.
- Agree upon a specific time frame for improvement.

From any discussion with your manager about some aspect of your performance that needs improvement, whenever possible you should come away with all three elements of a sound objective; that is, you should know what is to be done, how much must be done, and by when it should be done. Pursuing the overtime example, rather than agreeing that you will work to bring overtime usage down, you might agree to reduce overtime usage (the what) to no more than budgeted levels (the how much) by the end of the second quarter of the year (the when).

Negotiate Your Evaluation Score

Your performance appraisal goes into your personnel file and thus becomes part of your official record of employment. It will remain there as long as you remain with the organization, it will probably stay there long after you have left, and it will perhaps be accessed for reference purposes. Therefore, you have an interest in the indicated level of performance that becomes part of the official record. Also, if your organization operates a merit-pay program and if some portion of your merit increase depends on your evaluation score, you have an additional, as well as a more practical and immediate, interest in what goes into the record.

Regarding the commentary that might appear on your evaluation, do not be overly concerned with one or two apparent weak spots if the overall rendering of your performance is favorable on the whole. These days there is less and less likelihood of specific appraisal comments being used in references unless they are wholly positive. The most you are now likely to see about performance references is a check off to indicate that performance was, for example, above standard, at standard, or below standard.

Regarding an evaluation score, whatever that may be in terms of numeric or alphanumeric indicators according to your organization's appraisal system, your score will not result in long-run damage if it indicates your performance to be at or above your organization's defined level of standard performance. If there is money at stake, however, as in a merit-pay system that provides higher raises for higher evaluation scores, you might wish to challenge the scoring (diplomatically, of course) to determine whether you can improve the outcome of your appraisal.

Challenging your appraisal score falls solidly under the heading of nothing ventured, nothing gained. It cannot hurt to try to negotiate a slightly higher score, especially if you sincerely believe (without ego tripping) that you have done a better job than the score reflects and if you feel that you have done a reasonable job of convincing your manager that there are some important considerations he or she may have overlooked.

It is difficult to predict how your manager might react to your attempt to negotiate a higher evaluation score. Some managers will feel totally committed to the comments and scores they have set to paper before the appraisals are discussed, and they behave as though changing an evaluation score indicates weakness or indecisiveness on their part; some managers deliberately allow room for negotiation in their scoring simply to see whether certain employees will take the initiative to challenge them and ask for more; and still other managers, ordinarily those who are totally unthreatened by participative process, will recognize that employees have valid input to supply to their reviews and will thus remain open to new information. Regardless of the style of management you work under, however, unless you report to the most autocratic of managers (whose style you will recognize in an instant) you have nothing to lose by opening up the subject of a negotiated increase in your evaluation score.

When the shoe is on the other foot, be extremely careful how you react to an employee who tries to negotiate a better evaluation with you. It is easy to experience immediate resentment with the employee, especially with one you feel you have already rated justly or even generously. Some employees, especially those who do not fully understand performance appraisal, feel they are being downrated if their scores are anything less than perfect. Or they perhaps feel they are not making progress if their scores are not higher with each subsequent evaluation. You need to apply great care in sorting out these particular employees from those others who have valid, specific input to bring to the appraisal process. Be sufficiently open and broad minded to recognize that an employee you are evaluating will sometimes be able to legitimately point out things that you missed. In letting the negotiation work for an employee who has a valid point, you can demonstrate your belief in participative processes and can show that you are sufficiently flexible to change your mind when given additional valid information.

KNOWING THE SYSTEM

Everyone in the organization should know exactly how the appraisal system works. Everyone from the level of first-line supervisor on up also should know exactly how to apply the system to others. However, rarely does either condition exist completely throughout the organization.

All managers at all levels who appraise others should have received basic instruction in the use of the performance appraisal system, and this instruction should be periodically reinforced. In most organizations, however, it is common to find managers who have never received more direction in applying the system than they get from a single, rapid reading of the instructions. If you know your organization's appraisal system, truly know it inside out and are thoroughly familiar with how it is applied, you will make your own appraisal easier for yourself and your manager.

Aside from the mechanics of timing, the scheduling of interviews, and so on, the features that all employees should know and understand may be encapsulated within the following three considerations:

1. Every employee should know the criteria against which he or she will be evaluated. This means that all specific responsibilities, all specific tasks, and all specific kinds of behavior that will be evaluated should be known to the employee in advance, as should the standards of performance or the measurements that will be applied. In other words, the employees should be well aware of the expectations of the system.

2. Every employee should know how scores are applied to each individual element of an appraisal, exactly how the final score is tabulated, and what that overall score translates into in terms of an overall relative description of performance (such as standard, satisfactory, unsatisfactory, outstanding, or whatever descriptive terms your particular system uses).

3. It is of critical importance that every employee understand the difference between standard performance (or satisfactory performance, or whatever your system calls it) and average performance. Although many of us tend to think of performance in terms of averages, and tend to place ourselves somewhere relative to average, we remain better off if our appraisal system never involves the use of the term *average* at all. The average performance of a work group is just that; it is the average of the overall scores of a number of people. However, standard performance—that performance level implicit in doing what one is expected to do in a reasonable manner with expected results under reasonable supervision—tends over the long run to be the lowest level of performance prevalent in the organization. After all, someone who is performing below the standard of the job is not doing what he or she was hired to do, and substandard performance should have been dealt with along the way. (This is what the employment probation period and certain other corrective measures are for.) Therefore, true average performance in a work group will invariably lie somewhere above standard performance. However, people who do not have a problem with the use of the term *standard performance* may nevertheless, strange to say, have difficulty with the term *average* as applied to their performance. Most of us have the tendency to think of ourselves as no less than average and perhaps a bit better than average, and we may tend to react negatively to average. ("Me? Only average?") The focus of the system should be on at least maintaining standard performance and achieving above-standard performance as possible, without reference to averages. However, a great many employees see the terms *standard* or *satisfactory* and think of them as average; this notion must be corrected if appraisal is to work as intended.

KEEPING THE APPRAISAL ALIVE

Do not allow your performance evaluation to simply vanish into your manager's files never to be seen again until the following year when it is time for your next appraisal. Rather, once or twice during the year secure some time with your manager to talk about an item or two from your most recent appraisal. The item that ideally should surface at such an interim discussion would be one for which your manager had some legitimate criticism and had offered some guidance for corrective action. If you feel you have made progress on this item, or if it is an item for which you had agreed upon a shorter time span than one year for reexamination, this item is appropriate for an interim performance discussion. Another topic suited for an interim performance discussion would be one for which, although you were judged to be satisfactory at your last appraisal, you believe that you have shown significant improvement.

In point of fact, any aspect of your performance in which you believe you can make some honest improvement can be used as an opener for an interim performance discussion. If you set some modest improvement objectives for yourself—say two or three mini-objectives for which you have developed a reasonable statement of what, how much, and when—you can use these to initiate a performance discussion with your manager that can be far more than just an exercise in keeping communication lines open.

Do likewise for your employees without them having to suggest it. That is, schedule one or two sessions for each employee between performance appraisals to discuss a few points relating to each one's last appraisal. Until your employees become accustomed to this practice, give them plenty of advance notice as to which past appraisal points you would like to discuss. In this manner you will encourage your employees to think about serious efforts to improve at times other than appraisal times, and you might even discover that you have inspired them to do some self-improvement objective setting of their own.

A TRUE TWO-WAY STREET

Effective performance appraisal is a two-way street that carries considerable traffic in both directions. However, if left totally up to the evaluator at all times appraisal can become, as it often does, a purely mechanical process that can be almost totally one-way. In far too many traditional approaches, the process is active for the appraiser but passive for the employees being evaluated. To fulfill its maximum potential, appraisal should be very nearly as active from the bottom up as it is from the top down.

The guidelines presented in this chapter deal largely with ways in which you can take a more active role in your own performance appraisal. Having done everything you reasonably can do to take an active role in your own appraisal, it remains up to you to then apply a common-sense, golden-rule approach to appraisal overall: evaluate your employees in the manner in which you would like to be evaluated by your manager. Recall what was said earlier about the applicability of basic human needs to most people. Then appreciate that, as far as performance appraisal is concerned, the appraisal approaches (or lack thereof) that leave you frustrated and discouraged are very nearly identical to those that will leave your employees frustrated and discouraged. There may be times when you have to tell yourself that your employees deserve better than what you are receiving yourself.

As managers we acquire a great deal of what we know about management from our management role models, especially from our immediate superiors. However, we rarely should allow our role models to dictate all that we do. As we learn by example what we should be doing, we also should learn by example what we should avoid doing. As far as your own performance appraisal is concerned, develop the best appraisal relationship possible with your manager. Then address the elements of that relationship that are weak or absent, and do your best to ensure that each of your employees is given the opportunity to develop the kind of performance appraisal relationship that you yourself would like to enjoy.

Part II
The People Process:
Doing Effective Appraisals

4

Preparing to Appraise Performance

TIME TO DO IT RIGHT

Performance appraisal, like other techniques that busy managers must apply in the course of their work, is often entered into with inadequate preparation. Many evaluators have found it necessary to write and deliver appraisals with no preparation other than reading some printed instructions, perhaps even having to infer their instructions from the legends on an appraisal form.

The busy manager is often caught in the cycle of the activity trap: when it is necessary to do an appraisal it occurs to the manager that some proper instruction would be in order, but there is no time for instruction this time around. The manager's intention of seeking help between appraisals is swept aside by the normal crush of business, then suddenly it is again time to do an appraisal. As appraisal itself is found to be readily postponable under some conditions, so too is appraisal education postponable. As in so many other important management activities, it takes time to do it right—time that we are not readily willing to spend because of all of the demands on us. But when we fail to take the time to do it right initially, we are invariably forced to devote time in the future to resolving the resulting problems.

However, education of both appraiser and employee is necessary if performance appraisal is to have a chance of working as intended. The education of managers and the education of nonmanagers concerning appraisal will not necessarily be the same; they are, after all, on opposite sides of the process. But even though the nonmanagerial employee does not necessarily need to know how to do it, the employee should be able to understand how it is done.

As will be explored in greater detail in Chapter 17, one of the prevailing views of a performance appraisal system's legal acceptability is that the evaluator is provided with written instructions on how to complete the appraisal.[1] Written instructions, of course, are not nearly enough by themselves, but having the appraisal system's instructions in writing and distributed to evaluators is an essential start.

The essence of preparation for appraisal is communication. Regardless of the characteristics of any specific appraisal system, and regardless of the methods used to convey information about the system to appraiser and employee, for appraisal to have a realistic chance of working as intended evaluators and employees alike should have:

- a mutual understanding of the objectives of performance appraisal
- a common appreciation of the need to appraise performance
- similar expectations of the performance appraisal process as it applies in their organization

PREPARING THE APPRAISER

The best-prepared appraisers are those who have had an active role in the design and development of the appraisal system they are required to use. There is nothing to compare with "owning a piece of the system" for encouraging the appraiser to accept the system, believe in it, and apply it conscientiously. This advantage, however, resides with those managers who happened to be in the right position to become involved when the decision was made to institute or revamp an appraisal system. Most appraisers find that they are required to work with an appraisal system that was already in place when they assumed their positions.

As a task, appraisal is not easy. Judgment and subjectivity are involved, there are seemingly endless variables to account for, and the process has potentially serious consequences for employees. Knowing the potential consequences and feeling uneasy with criticizing others to begin with, the appraiser who also feels ill prepared or uncertain about how to proceed often looks for a stress-reducing path through the process. Therefore, in addition to learning how to implement the mechanics of the appraisal system the manager also must learn how to deal with his or her own emotions.

This book cannot explain how to overcome the emotional barriers to appraisal in all appraisers for all time. Chances are this cannot be done. Appraisal requires occasional criticism; appraisal sometimes requires working out conflicts between manager and employee. For reasons that lie well beyond the scope of this discussion, some people will always remain uneasy about criticizing others or coming into conflict with others. But even though removal of all emotional barriers to appraisal cannot be guaranteed, it is possible to ensure that these emotional barriers are reduced to a practical minimum. This is done through education; the appraiser who feels well prepared and reasonably certain as to how to proceed will experience less stress from the process.

The following discussion about preparing the appraiser assumes the existence of a written procedure for accomplishing performance appraisals.

Unfortunately, such a procedure does not always exist, and in some organizations where the procedure does exist—after a fashion, out of date, and largely ignored—not every evaluator knows about it. If an up-to-date procedure does not exist in writing, top management, through human resources, should be encouraged to provide one not only as an essential aid to appraisers but also as one of the necessary features of a legally defensible appraisal system.[2]

The Appraiser's Training Needs

There are several reasons why it is crucial for the appraiser to be well trained in use of the appraisal system and thoroughly grounded in the system's guiding principles:

- to ensure that each employee is evaluated correctly, fairly, and as objectively as possible
- to ensure consistency of application from employee to employee and department to department
- to enable managers to fully use the system for performance improvement and personnel development
- to ensure that appraisal is communicated as a positive process that, while relatively formal, is a small but essential part of the continuing relationship between manager and employee

Training in performance appraisal should be provided:

- to all new appraisers, those persons new to management or new to the organization's system who have yet to appraise employee performance under this system (This training should be a prerequisite to the new manager's first use of the system, perhaps provided as part of a new-manager orientation.)
- to all appraisers on a refresher basis, periodically reinforcing the users' knowledge of the system and as far as possible ensuring continued consistency of application
- to all appraisers whenever there are significant changes to the system, such as changes in measurement standards or changes in the manner in which job description tasks are translated into evaluation criteria

Training ordinarily will be provided or coordinated by the organization's human resource department or training department. The instructors frequently will be the human resource practitioners who are responsible for administering the appraisal system or professional instructors assigned to training. However, some of the best instructors for performance appraisal are working line managers—active users of the appraisal system—who are prepared with instructional techniques. Frequently it appears that the detailed ins and outs and subtleties of performance appraisal are best conveyed to others by those who have had significant hands-on experience with the process.

Often outside consultants are involved in appraisal training, especially consultants who have been engaged to participate in the design of a new or revised system. However, the training (and, for that matter, the system design) should not be left solely to the consultants. The better consultants will draw the organization's management into the design process and will concentrate most of their training efforts on preparing internal trainers to do the continuing work of communicating the system to its users.

Striving for Consistency

One of the most important words to arise from among the several aims of performance appraisal training is consistency. Every manager who uses the organization's appraisal system can influence how that system is applied. The appraisal system in a large health care organization can have hundreds of users; in even a small organization a significant percentage of the employee population can be evaluators. The opportunity for variations in system application is considerable; thus the need for regular attention to ensuring consistency of application from employee to employee and department to department.

Consistency in application and administration of the appraisal system is crucial to the defensibility of the system in the event of legal challenge. Courts may at times have difficulty deciding on issues of communication, job relatedness, and the like, but experience shows that the courts can easily recognize inconsistency.[3] Consistency needs to be a constant concern; the same rules must be applied in the same way to all persons who are similarly situated.

The Training Topics

Depending on the level of personnel to be evaluated—rank-and-file employees, supervisors and managers, technical or professional workers, etc.—some or all of the following topics should be included in the appraiser's training:

System Overview

All employees (rank-and-file workers as well as those who are expected to formally evaluate the performance of others) should receive an overview of the performance appraisal system, preferably as part of new-employee orientation. This should include introduction to the purposes of appraisal, familiarization with the written appraisal procedure, a review of the appraisal form and its use, and a review of the timetable and deadlines that are part of the total process.

Employees who are elevated to management from the ranks should experience this system overview again as part of their new manager orientation and preparation.

Legal Aspects of Appraisal

All appraisers should be educated in the potential legal problems related to performance appraisal (see Chapter 17). This can be a form of legal overview, imparting the knowledge that several dimensions of appraisal—the need for consistency of application, the need for objectivity, the need to be specific, the need to stay focused on performance—are filled with legal pitfalls. Subsequent training then teaches the appraisal process in a manner that takes into account the requirements of legally defensible appraisal.

Writing Objective Appraisals

Total objectivity is a theoretical ideal. Objectivity can only be approached, and then only through practice.[4] Therefore, there should be a great deal of emphasis placed on writing the kinds of comments that are necessary to support the scores given to various aspects of performance. No appraisal system is even remotely worthy of the name unless it requires that scores be backed up with words.

Actual appraisal language should be critiqued and rewritten in an active workshop that provides hands-on writing experience and includes the opportunity to review appraisal language before and after. Efforts in these writing activities should be focused along two lines:

1. All written comments should describe elements of job performance, not behavior or characteristics of the person. For example, in regard to an employee whose required inservice education attendance has been unpredictable and generally unacceptable, one would not make a comment like: "Cannot be depended on to attend required inservice classes," because this statement describes the person in what can be seen as an aspect of personality (undependable). Rather than saying the employee cannot be depended on to do something, the appraiser needs to say simply that the employee did not do it. This latter statement puts the attention on the appropriate issue—the results of the employee's behavior (that is, the employee's performance).

2. All comments of a critical nature need to be specific and as factually defensible as possible. The comment, "Often absent from required inser-

vice classes," although properly focusing on performance rather than person, the statement is insufficiently general (how frequent is often?). Rather, the evaluator more appropriately should write: "Missed four required inservice education classes (30%) in the preceding 12 months," with two kinds of information available in the backup material—the required level of attendance (the "standard"), and the exact dates of the classes the employee missed.

More will be said about the written language of performance appraisal in Chapter 5.

Conducting the Appraisal Interview

The initial concern for the appraisal interview is that it take place at all; somehow a great many appraisal interviews never take place, especially those associated with so-called routine favorable evaluations, or if they do take place they consist of a bit of social chatter and perhaps an "Any questions?" inquiry.

Beyond simply ensuring that the interview happens, the appraiser should be utilizing the interview to serve the objectives of performance appraisal. The appraisal interview ordinarily will be a problem-solving type of interview (even when there may be no apparent problems to solve), making this encounter considerably different from, for example, an employment interview, which is essentially an information-gathering type of interview.

As an integral part of instruction in appraisal interviewing, the evaluator should receive training in active listening techniques.

Specific information about conducting the appraisal interview appears in Chapter 7.

Management by Objectives (MBO) and Joint Target Setting

At the very least every appraiser should receive basic instruction in how to help employees develop improvement plans and how to set goals and formulate objectives. The appraiser must learn to guide the employee in the establishment of goals and objectives that the employee owns but that remain consistent with the objectives of the department and thus the organization.

Goals and objectives sometimes may not be necessary in dealing with some employees, primarily entry level nontechnical or nonprofessional workers, who consistently function satisfactorily. However, joint target setting (the development of mutually agreed-on work performance targets), and perhaps even formal management by objectives (MBO), may be appropriate for:

• technical and professional nonmanagerial employees

- all levels of managerial personnel
- any employee who asks the appraiser for help in determining what he or she can do to improve performance.

At the heart of instruction in determining goals and objectives should be the wherewithal to guide evaluators in ensuring that all objectives accepted and pursued fulfill the three conditions of an appropriate objective in that they include:

- what is to be done
- how much is to be done
- when it is to be done

It is because of nonspecific objectives that a great many target-setting and MBO activities fail. For example, consider a supervisor's objective that states: "To reduce overtime usage in the unit." This objective includes the *what* only; since there is no indication of *how much* or *when*, there is no realistic way of determining whether the objective has been met satisfactorily. With this kind of open-ended target one can always rationalize a supposed degree of success (or failure). This weakens the entire process. However, if the objective states, "To reduce overtime usage (what) by 25% (how much) within six months (when)," it is possible to look at results after six months and judge fairly readily whether the objective was truly met. Although *what* accompanied by just *how much* makes a better target than *what* alone, without the *when* it remains open-ended. Promising to reduce overtime by 25% within 3 months, for example, would be a far more ambitious objective than promising to reduce overtime by 25% within 12 or 15 months.

Information that can be used to guide appraiser training in this aspect of preparation appears in Chapter 15.

PREPARING THE EMPLOYEE

No decision process is more critical to an employee's career than performance measurement. This creates a persuasive argument for employee participation in the process.[5] Although there may be only limited opportunities to involve certain entry level employees, and there will always be some employees (usually also at entry levels) who do not wish to become especially involved, the health care work force includes many well educated and generally sophisticated employees who are capable of constructive involvement in performance appraisal.

The two keys to employee preparation for appraisal are knowledge and participation. Knowledge and participation are the most effective cures for classic employee resistance arising from two common sources: employees resist that which is unknown to them; and employees resist that which they perceive as uncontrollable by them.

Absolutely all employees can be provided with the knowledge needed to help them overcome much of their resistance to appraisal; most employees can also be given the added incentive of involvement in some aspect of the total appraisal process.

System Overview and Appraisal's Objectives

It was stated earlier that all employees initially need to receive an overview of the organization's appraisal process. This should be accomplished when each employee is relatively new to the organization, perhaps at general orientation to the organization or at departmental orientation. This overview should include clear, concise definitions of the objectives of performance appraisal. Right from the start each employee should be able to understand why appraisal is done and generally how it is done.

System Characteristics

An effective performance appraisal system requires evaluators to communicate job standards and other criteria to employees before the evaluation period begins. This way employees know what constitutes acceptable performance and an evaluator can then assess performance more objectively. Therefore, in addition to learning the objectives of appraisal, each employee should learn the features of the system as they affect his or her evaluation, specifically:

- the basis on which his or her performance will be evaluated; generally, this includes the job description elements or other expressions of required job performance that make up the job's performance criteria (the "vertical scale" of the appraisal)
- the meaning of the measures to be applied; for example, the simplest possible definitions of the degree-of-success judgments (satisfactory, excellent, etc.), or what constitutes having not met, met, or exceeded a standard, including absolute objective measures when available (the "horizontal scale" of the appraisal)

In brief, the employee needs to know management's expectations of his or her performance.

System Operations

Each employee requires certain information about the manner in which the appraisal system functions. Specifically, the employee should know:

- the frequency and timing of appraisal, including the approximate date when he or she can expect to receive an appraisal
- the uses to which performance appraisal results may be put (for example, in apportioning wage increases or in making decisions concerning promotion, demotion, transfer, layoff, etc.)
- the extent to which an employee's appraisal results can be shared with others (for example, for internal and external references)

Self Appraisal

Each employee to whom self appraisal may apply should know that he or she may be asked about the possibility of performing a self appraisal. It is recommended that self appraisal be presented as an option that the employee may either exercise or decline. Some employees are sufficiently upset by the prospect of appraising themselves—worrying about whether they will sell themselves short with self-ratings below the manager's evaluation, or create poor impressions with self-ratings higher than the manager's evaluation—that any potential value from self appraisal is wiped out by the negative effects on the employees.

Additional Opportunity for Involvement

Beyond knowing whether self appraisal might be recommended, each employee should know the extent to which his or her further involvement in the appraisal process is possible. As covered in subsequent chapters, employee involvement can take a number of forms depending on employee level and degree of job sophistication. Additional employee involvement opportunities might include:

- developing, reworking, or otherwise revising the employee's own job description
- developing the criteria on which the employee will be assessed and measures by which performance will be gauged
- developing goals and objectives for improvement and negotiating these to agreement with the evaluator.

At the very least every employee should know that he or she can comment on the evaluation for the record. This represents participation in the appraisal process in its most elementary form, but it is generally available to all employees: the employee can enter comments or opinions (positive, negative, or otherwise) on the appraisal form and should be encouraged to do so. The employee should be encouraged to sign the evaluation but should understand that signing does not necessarily mean agreement or acceptance, but simply an acknowledgment that the employee has received and discussed the appraisal.

Each employee also should be advised of any process that exists for appealing some aspect of an appraisal with which he or she might not agree.

NO-SURPRISES APPRAISAL

If distrust, suspicion or strong uncertainty exist in the minds of employees—about the appraisal policy, the appraisal process, or the use of the appraisal results—openness will be discouraged.[6] Further, all chances of open communication with employees concerning appraisal will be destroyed if the manager practices "gotcha!" appraisal, saving negative incidents or harsh criticisms until appraisal time. There are few managerial actions more likely than "gotcha!" appraisal to arouse distrust, suspicion, or uncertainty among employees.

There are two bases for no-surprises appraisal. This first is what the past few pages have been all about: employee information about appraisal and how it is done. The other lies in the relationship between manager and subordinate; that is, between evaluator and employee. A theme that continually surfaces in this book, first noted in the preface, is that the most important element in appraising performance is the relationship that exists between manager and employee. If the good and the bad, the targets hit and the goals missed, the triumphs and the failures, are all dealt with in the relationship as they occur, and never saved up to surface only at appraisal time, the major component of no-surprises appraisal is covered. The actual appraisal will be a mere formality because employee and manager will know where they stand with each other at all times.

NOTES

1. The Bureau of National Affairs, "Four Elements Held Crucial in EEO Performance Appraisal Cases," *White Collar Report*, vol. 57, no. 2 (January 16, 1985) p. 38.
2. *Ibid.*
3. Ronald G. Wells, "Guidelines for Effective and Defensible Performance Appraisal Systems," *Personnel Journal*, vol. 61, no. 10, p. 780.
4. Martin G. Friedman, "10 Steps to Objective Appraisals," *Personnel Journal*, vol. 65, no. 6 (June 1986) p. 71.
5. Mark R. Edwards, "A Joint Effort Leads to Accurate Appraisals," *Personnel Journal*, vol. 69, no. 6, p. 124.
6. Wells, p. 781.

5

Doing the Appraisal: The Writeup

NEVER A ONE-SHOT JOB

In the otherwise extensive periodical literature about performance appraisal there is little said about actually writing appraisals. Implicit in many papers and articles about appraisal is the notion that the appraiser fills out a form. In fact, some treatments of appraisal refer not to the performance appraisal system or performance appraisal as a process but rather refer to the use of the performance appraisal form. A proper appraisal can be said to be thought out and written out; it cannot be described as simply filled out.

Writing an employee's performance appraisal should never occur as an isolated task. There needs to be more involved than simply sitting down and dashing off an appraisal. Before words land on lines or in spaces and before numbers or check marks drop into boxes, a considerable amount of thought and a modest amount of effort need to be expended over a period of time.

The necessary thought and effort have to be put into learning about the employee's performance and establishing the means of retrieving what has been learned when it is required. Few evaluators have memories sufficiently good to allow them to write a fair and thorough appraisal solely by unaided recall, especially considering that most appraisals cover a full year's activity.

FOLLOWING THE REQUIREMENTS OF THE SYSTEM

There is usually a time frame specified in which the evaluator is expected to write a particular appraisal. Under a system in which all employees are evaluated at the same time of year, the evaluator may be given a certain time—one month is fairly common—to complete the paper portion of all appraisals. (An appraisal is never fully complete until it is discussed with the employee; however, this chapter deals primarily with creating the appraisal document.)

When the organization's appraisal system calls for evaluation on or about an employee's employment anniversary date, the evaluator is usually given a few weeks' advance notice of an appraisal falling due. Whether all-at-once or anniversary date, however, it is important to faithfully follow your system's time requirements (see Chapter 6).

It is also necessary to utilize the appraisal form completely by providing all information that is called for and filling out all applicable spaces. The majority of appraisal forms allow for some written commentary in support of numeric scores, but a great many evaluators simply check boxes or enter numbers in spaces and neglect to back up these marks with words.

Be wary of any appraisal system that uses checks or numbers only, without written comments. It is of such importance to back up scores with comments that we can safely say that any worthwhile appraisal system will encourage, if not require, performance assessments to be expressed verbally as well as numerically. Yet time and again many evaluators will enter numbers or check off boxes while ignoring the spaces provided for written commentary. Or, sometimes even more troublesome, evaluators will enter written comments that are inconsistent with the scores that have been checked. It is not uncommon, for example, to find a check mark for satisfactory on some aspect of performance backed up with a comment like: "Needs to improve in (some aspect of the job duty)." Such inconsistencies cause employee confusion and often cloud real issues when an appraisal winds up in court.

GATHERING APPRAISAL INFORMATION

It is no secret that many managers are uncomfortable doing performance appraisals. One of the reasons often cited for evaluators' discomfort is that they do not know enough about the people who work for them to assess their performance accurately. It is claimed frequently that many supervisors are so busy trying to do their jobs that they are unable to spend enough time observing those who work for them.[1]

Consider, however, what the heart of a supervisor's job really consists of, or what it really should consist of—the business of getting the work of the department done *primarily* through the efforts of the employees. Management at all levels will always be the process of getting things done through people. With the exception of the occasional supervisor who is truly overburdened with non-supervisory tasks, those supervisors who feel they are too busy to be thoroughly familiar with what their employees are doing are functioning ineffectively. At the very least they are failing to delegate properly. Thus the claim of "too busy" is in most cases no more than a lame excuse.

The effective supervisor will be well aware of what each employee is doing most of the time. It remains only for the supervisor to approach the collection and retention of performance related information in a logical manner.

Anecdotal Note Files

It can be extremely helpful for the manager to maintain a file on each employee. However, there is certainly no need for the manager to keep everything related to an employee and essentially duplicate the organization's personnel file for that employee. The focus of the manager's employee file should be anecdotal notes of observations, incidents, and encounters that have a bearing on the employee's work performance and observance of policies and work rules.

The best way to retain a bit of information that will influence an employee's next appraisal is to write it down. The evaluator should do just that throughout the course of the year, making note of both positive and negative occurrences that should or logically would be reflected in an appraisal. This can be described as the manager's personal exception reporting in its simplest form; nothing is noted regarding expected performance or behavior, but exceptions, both welcome and unwelcome, are noted for future consideration in an appraisal.

Exceptions, again both welcome and unwelcome, should be dealt with to the extent they deserve when they occur. Although a number of events that occur throughout the year might be reflected later in an evaluation, the evaluation itself should hold no surprises for the employee. A breach of rules or policy or an occurrence of substandard performance should be acknowledged when it happens, with the appropriate disciplinary or corrective action taken. Similarly, a commendation or an instance of exemplary performance should be acknowledged at the time it occurs. Retaining certain information that might be reflected later in an appraisal in no way relieves the manager of the responsibility for communicating with the employee on a timely basis.

Anecdotal note files are recommended strongly for accumulating performance appraisal information. However, because there are hazards associated with keeping such files, it is necessary to approach the creation and maintenance of such files in a more or less defensive manner. Most of the hazards presented by anecdotal note files are legal in nature (see Chapter 17), but some relate simply to day-to-day operating concerns. Following are some recommendations for anecdotal note files:

- Every time you set pen or pencil to paper, first put the date on the page. Whether generating anecdotal notes or any other formal or informal document, the date is extremely important. Inconvenience, confusion, and even damage of various sorts can result when undated documents have to be called on at a later date.

- Do not go overboard to the extent that you seem to be continually writing something about one or more of your employees. Stick to the true exceptions, and keep your written comments brief. You should be writing clear, concise passages that are more memory triggers than complete recountings. You need facts, not volume, and you do not want to create the impression among your employees that you are constantly writing things down about them.

- Make all of your notes as objective as possible and keep them completely free from labeling and name calling. Your anecdotal notes are no place to unload your frustrations with an employee or express unsupported opinions of a person's character or value. A helpful rule to remember is to put nothing on paper that you would be ashamed to see made public. Keep in mind that even your most private working files legally can be made public under certain circumstances.
- Periodically purge your anecdotal note files of outdated and irrelevant material. When notes you have accumulated have been worked into an appraisal, purge the notes. Formal documents, such as letters of commendation concerning employees, can go into the employees' personnel files, but your informal notes should be destroyed once they are merged into an evaluation. Even if not used in an appraisal writeup, informal notes should be destroyed after a reasonable length of time. However, if a legal action has been instituted concerning a particular employee, do not discard any documents pertaining in any way to that employee.

WRITING THE APPRAISAL

The majority of the problems emerging from the written portion of most performance appraisals are embodied in appraisal comments that:

- are presented in inappropriate writing styles
- are improperly focused on person instead of on performance
- do not accurately reflect the evaluator's observations and opinions
- are weighed down with subjectivity and loaded with potential emotional triggers

Writing Style

Performance appraisal comments should be written in a lean, spare style that wastes no words and employs a necessary minimum of adjectives and qualifiers.

Most appraisal forms provide a specific amount of space in which to provide the comments that back up each score. Although most evaluators should be aware that they are usually free to continue their comments on additional pages, it is the rare evaluator who actually does so. Most evaluators who use up the available comment space simply quit writing at that point. And although they may not be fully aware of what they are doing, in just filling up the available space many evaluators write wordy, rambling prose that says little of substance but fills the space, thus supposedly satisfying the requirements of the system.

This is not to say that appraisal comments must be written in "telegraphese"— that is, "Results good—no problems." Simple, declarative sentences, carrying specific information, are usually adequate. Each comment should support why the score on the criterion to which it relates was given. For example, consider one criterion on the appraisal for an employee described as a financial secretary:

> *Initiate all insurance billings within one week (5 work days) of visit.*
> *(Expectation: 99%.)* (This criterion is accompanied by a standard in
> the form of a designated level of acceptable performance. It is far
> easier for employee and evaluator alike when both know what consti-
> tutes acceptable performance in absolute terms.)

In assessing performance against this single requirement the evaluator filled the comment space and ran into and down the margin of the form to write:

> (The employee) is almost always very timely in initiating billings, and
> is almost always within the one week requirement. She experienced a
> bit of a back up during two holiday weeks, but that was understand-
> able because of the days off. Not counting short work weeks and one
> brief illness, she was more like 99.9% accurate in living up to the
> expectation.

Writing in a lean, spare style, the evaluator might better have said:

> (The employee) initiates insurance billings within one week of the
> visit nearly 100% of the time, exceeding the job standard. [These
> words would properly accompany a score number or check that indi-
> cated above-standard performance.]

The task of writing appropriate evaluation comments is the same as the task of writing most other notes, letters, memoranda, and other documents in the business setting. Effective business writing is a skill generally acquired through practice. There is little the average manager writes that cannot be improved by thoughtful editing or rewriting; one can improve at writing appraisal comments simply be refusing to accept one's own first words that land on the paper.

To begin improving at writing appraisal comments, treat your initial render-ing of any employee's appraisal as a first draft. Refine that draft by cutting out excess adjectives and qualifiers, eliminating duplication, replacing roundabout phrases with fewer words (for example, why say "due to the fact that" when you mean "because"?), and in general describing the person's performance in a few simple words.

A good source of practice material can be found in the past appraisals that you and other evaluators have written. Try critiquing a number of past appraisals with the foregoing comments in mind, and consult a good writing reference book for further advice. Probably the most valuable single reference is the widely used *The Elements of Style* by Strunk and White, which provides a wealth of straightforward writing assistance in fewer than 80 total pages.[2]

Focus of Comments

As alluded to repeatedly throughout this book, many earlier approaches to performance appraisal encouraged—even required—assessment of the person, and not necessarily the person's performance. It has become increasingly clear, however, that any appraisal system that permits comments to focus on what the person is rather than on what the person does is creating problems.

As the vertical scale weaknesses of appraisal are gradually corrected and references to personality characteristics give way to reliance on task-based evaluation criteria, evaluators will be more and more encouraged to focus on performance rather than person.

One way to help stay away from an unwarranted focus of comments on the person is to remember to place the proper emphasis on the person's behavior. Performance, whether standard, substandard, or above standard, results from behavior; likewise, observance or nonobservance of policies or work rules results from behavior. The evaluator is usually on safe ground when dealing factually with the results of behavior. It is when attempting to assign cause to the behavior that the evaluator enters dangerous territory.

Consider the following passage that appeared on the appraisal of a technician: "Your stubbornness has continued to cause problems, as exhibited by at least two specific incidents of open disagreement with department management."

The evaluator who wrote this comment probably thought doing so was fully appropriate, especially when including reference to specific incidents. However, what the evaluator actually did was observe the results of behavior— the incidents of disagreement—and attempted to infer the cause, supposedly the employee's stubbornness.

It is the almost natural but completely unwarranted leap from result to cause that has the evaluator immediately assessing some aspect of personality. The personality related inference is unwarranted because the vast majority of evaluators are totally unqualified to render valid personality judgments. Again, the only correct focus for evaluation is what the person did—actions or the results of actions.

Inaccurate Reporting

A great many problems are experienced because of appraisal comments that do not accurately reflect the evaluator's true observations and opinions. Inaccurate appraisal reporting is customarily manifested as:

- leniency in both scoring and comments, as the evaluator, for any number of reasons, rates the employee more favorably than deserved
- disagreement between scoring and comments, with numerical scoring reflecting either more or less favorable assessment than the written comments

Regarding leniency in appraisal, one of the most frequent sources of appraisal-related problems is the no-fault appraisal—a satisfactory or otherwise neutral or perhaps even better than satisfactory appraisal—of an employee whom the manager actually considers to be performing or behaving in substandard fashion. In actuality a considerable number of employees who are considered marginal are carried along with lenient appraisals.

Lenient appraisals usually occur because of evaluators' discomfort with the performance appraisal process, discomfort that exists for a number of reasons touched on in preceding chapters, including:

- lack of appropriate evaluator training (An evaluator who is not fully knowledgeable of all aspects of the appraisal process will tend to compensate for this lack with leniency.)
- lack of sufficient knowledge of employees' activities (A manager whose job emphasis is misplaced, resulting in insufficient knowledge of employees' work performance, will likewise tend to compensate with leniency.)
- unwillingness on the part of the evaluator to make an assessment that could affect an employee's pay or continued employment, or simply unwillingness to experience an employee's disappointment or displeasure

The inconsistent appraisal, in which scoring and comments do not agree, is simply a variation on the lenient appraisal. In most such cases the leniency is embodied primarily in the numerical scoring; the scoring will indicate standard or even above standard performance but the comments will convey the impression of less than acceptable performance in some dimensions. Since it is usually the score that features more prominently in the personnel record and perhaps in the compensation system, in this manner the evaluator avoids getting the employee into serious trouble and perhaps ensures a pay increase, but also seemingly fulfills an obligation to dispense due criticism.

Inconsistent or lenient appraisals send a misleading message. They tell the employee either: "You're doing okay, period," or, "There are some small things you might fix, but you're generally doing fine." This misleading message is unfair to the employee and dangerous to the evaluator. Evaluations accrue year after year in an employee's personnel file. When a manager has finally "had it up to here" with a chronically marginal employee, and the manager has nothing to fall back on but a file full of satisfactory appraisals, most efforts at correction are thwarted and potential legal problems arise.

Subjectivity and Emotionalism

The core problem of performance appraisal is the necessity for human judg-ment to control the process. Some of the more highly quantified approaches to performance appraisal have actually been attempts to eliminate managerial judgment from the process. However, eliminating judgment from appraisal is all but impossible except in cases involving highly structured, repetitive, exter-nally controlled jobs in which there are only two possible outcomes—the employee either does or does not do as expected (as in some assembly line man-ufacturing activities where it is only necessary to count attendance and physical output to assess performance).

Judgment remains very much a part of modern performance appraisal, espe-cially for the kinds of jobs that most health care workers hold. Modern direc-tions in appraisal are not intended to eliminate the need for judgment; rather, they are intended to reduce the scope of judgment applied in assessing task per-formance, to aid or reduce judgment through the use of selected objective meas-ures, and to ensure that necessary judgments are performance related and suffi-ciently subdivided to force independent consideration of many dimensions of performance. In brief, an appropriate modern appraisal is not a broad, sweeping judgment of an employee; it is the net result of a number of narrow, specific, well-defined judgments of an employee's performance.

The constant presence of the need for judgment means also the constant dan-ger of excessive subjectivity. A great many subjective assessments, positive as well as negative, have no legitimate place in a performance appraisal. The assessment that cannot be backed up at least partially with fact has no legitimate place in a performance appraisal. Far better to simply relate all assessments in one way or another to the known standards of the job or to management's expectations of the employee, judging whether the employee met, failed to meet, or exceeded those standards or expectations. The more pure subjectivity there is in an appraisal, the less credible the appraisal and the more readily it can be disputed.

Emotionalism in appraisals can also trigger problems, the more obvious of which are likely to arise from negative commentary. The worst instances involve what essentially can be described as name calling; the evaluator applies an emotionally rooted label to which the employee subsequently reacts emotionally. For example, referring to an employee as careless, unmotivated, or uncooperative usually will trigger negative feelings on the part of the employee. However, much potential emotionalism can be avoided by framing comments in a way that clearly focuses on the person's performance without inference of the likely causes within the person.

It is also prudent to avoid the use of unsupportable general statements to describe employee performance or conduct. One can safely say that two of the worst words to use in describing the actions of another are always and never, as in "You always do this," or "You never do that." Rarely are such statements true in an absolute sense, and if at all negative they usually serve only to raise emotional barriers to effective communication.

CRITICISM: THE TWO-EDGED SWORD

Honest performance appraisal occasionally involves criticism. Criticism is upsetting to both appraiser and employee; it is discomforting to deliver for many people (thus more of the pressure toward leniency in appraisal), and it is understandably discomforting to the recipient. It is a two-edged sword that can cut sender and receiver alike.

As a word in the English language, criticism carries a generally negative connotation. We attempt to ameliorate this negative connotation by modifying the word with a particular adjective: constructive. Indeed, all legitimate criticism should be constructive; that is, it also should embody the means of correcting the offending performance or behavior. In proper performance appraisal the means of correction is the job standard itself or an indication of how to achieve the job standard.

Constructive or not, however, criticism remains criticism; regardless of how considerately it is delivered it retains the capacity to offend or disappoint.

In performance appraisal it is extremely important to criticize when criticism is due. However, criticism in appraisal must always be completely honest, as specific as possible, and fully objective, and must always be delivered— whether in writing or in person—with consideration and compassion.

NOTES

1. Paul R. Reed and Mark J. Kroll, "A Two-Perspective Approach to Performance Appraisal," *Personnel*, vol. 62, no. 10 (October 1985) p. 52.

2. William Strunk, Jr. and E.B. White, *The Elements of Style*, 2nd ed. (New York: Macmillan Publishing Co., Inc., 1972).

6

Timing: The Single Appraisal and the Many*

FREQUENCY AND TIMING

Timing is a critical factor in performance appraisal in at least two distinctly different senses. For the manager who must make performance appraisals, the timing of any one employee's appraisal relative to all other employees' appraisals is important. For the employee who is evaluated, the timing of the actual appraisal relative to the employee's expectations is likewise important. In either or both senses, timing can either strengthen or weaken the effectiveness of the organization's appraisal system. This chapter will explore the implications of timing in the performance appraisal process.

Before embarking on a discussion of the timing of performance appraisal, however, the frequency of appraisal should be addressed. The overwhelming majority of health care organizations evaluate the performance of each employee once each year. Although semiannual appraisal is no longer as popular as it once was, a few organizations continue to evaluate all employees semiannually rather than annually.

Which frequency is best? When considered idealistically, focusing largely on motivational aspects of performance appraisal, the semiannual appraisal is probably more valuable. After all, appraisal does, or at least should, require some serious one-to-one exploration of aspects of an employee's performance, thus serving to provide the employee with more formal feedback concerning both positive and negative aspects of performance.

However, performance appraisal, properly and conscientiously applied, is a time-consuming process. Even in organizations in which appraisal is done only once each year, appraisal may loom as a nearly overwhelming task. Consider all of the activity that must go into a well-developed appraisal: the thoughtful consideration of the notes that should be kept from one appraisal to the next; the actual development of the appraisal, perhaps through a draft or

---

*An earlier version of this chapter first appeared as Charles R. McConnell, "When Performance Appraisal Happens: Timing is Everything," *The Health Care Supervisor,* vol. 9, no. 2 (December, 1990).

two; the scoring of the appraisal, by whatever means may be available or required; the actual appraisal discussion; and the necessary follow up that might be indicated by the results of the appraisal. Then consider the fact that all of this work is multiplied by the number of employees working under the appraiser's immediate supervision. It is not unusual to encounter some supervisors (such as the head nurse of a sizeable unit) who have to do 20, 25, or more appraisals.

Thus once-per-year appraisal has become more common than semiannual appraisal. But once-per-year appraisal can be perfectly adequate as long as everything in the supervisor-employee relationship that should happen from one appraisal to the next does in fact happen. As previously suggested, in semiannual appraisal the employee is assured of reasonably detailed performance feedback at more frequent intervals than is possible with annual appraisal. However, if performance appraisal time is the only time the employee receives detailed performance feedback, then semiannual appraisal is only marginally more valuable than annual appraisal.

Regardless of the frequency with which it is done, performance appraisal should hold no surprises for the employee. As frequently stated and implied throughout this book, if the continuing relationship between manager and employee is everything that it should be at all times, then appraisal, regardless of when it occurs, will be a mere formality as far as performance feedback is concerned because both parties will already know where they stand with each other.

Within the framework of a common once-per-year performance appraisal system, a few variations involving interim appraisals might be encountered. For example, it is fairly common to evaluate a new employee at the end of an initial probationary period (sometimes three months, in some instances six months) before that person enters the regular annual appraisal cycle. Also, a special interim appraisal might be done on an employee who is under serious consideration for promotion or who might have suddenly exhibited marked performance difficulties that ought to be addressed before the next scheduled appraisal arrives.

For the sake of consistency of presentation, the following discussion of the timing of performance appraisal will assume an appraisal frequency of once per year throughout. Also, it should be kept in mind that probationary appraisals may take place and a few special-purpose appraisals may occur between regularly scheduled evaluations.

ALL AT ONCE OR OTHERWISE?

The two common approaches to the timing of performance appraisal are: evaluate everyone in the organization at once, at a single scheduled time of the year; or appraise each employee on some regularly recurring date, commonly the anniversary of the person's employment with the organization or the anniversary of transfer into the employee's current position. Some managers prefer one approach, some managers prefer the other. Although a considerable body of experience suggests that more managers prefer the anniversary-date approach to the all-at-once approach, a considerable number of organizations have remained with the all-at-once approach. This discussion primarily promotes anniversary-date appraisal to the extent of advocating the abandonment of the all-at-once appraisal process, but it will also give full weight not only to the strengths of both approaches but also to the difficulties inherent in attempting to dislodge a solidly entrenched all-at-once appraisal process.

Comparing Approaches: People Considerations

From the perspective of the *individual* employee, anniversary-date appraisal comes across as more personalized and thus appears to be favored (or at least tolerated) more than the all-at-once approach. An employee ordinarily knows the scheduled review date well in advance, and thus knows that sometime near that scheduled date a review will be written up and an appraisal discussion will take place soon thereafter. Also, if there is a merit pay increment involved, in most cases the employee knows that a raise will occur within a pay period or two of when the appraisal takes place. The employee is likely to experience a sense of currentness. That is, the appraisal is written about current performance, the discussion deals with current performance, and the merit increment is seen as a award for current performance.

When all appraisals are done at once, however, the individual employee is less likely to experience a sense of currentness. Consider, for example, the timetable at work in an organization of nearly 3,000 employees that awards its merit increases on or immediately after January 1 of each year. Appraisal forms and timetables are distributed by the human resource department in the middle of September, with instructions for evaluators to have their appraisals written and approved by the next level of management by the end of the third week of October. The last week of October is allowed for dealing with stragglers and running preliminary distributions of scores, then inconsistencies and apparent problems are dealt with, and evaluators are given all of November in which to schedule and conduct their appraisal interviews.

After allowing another few days to round up those who have not remained on schedule, a portion of December is then consumed in determining how the money available for increases should be distributed according to evaluation scores. Following an announcement late in December, everyone's merit increase becomes effective as of the first pay period of the new year.

Is so much time truly necessary? Experience has shown that this much time is indeed necessary. Although there are some evaluators who will always run late for a variety of reasons regardless of the system, we cannot forget that the all-at-once approach requires some evaluators to evaluate many people in a relatively short time. To extend an example cited earlier, it is conceivable that a particular head nurse will have to develop 25 or more appraisals in a five or six week period, all in addition to doing her regular work. When viewed in this manner, five or six weeks does not sound like too long a time to write evaluations. However, to the individual employee the time may seem extended indeed. The employee might talk with the evaluator in November concerning what he or she sees as a "snapshot" of performance as of late September or early October, and then have to wait until after the first of January for the "reward" to arrive. Thus the more time that is allowed to elapse between the three major events—written appraisal, discussion, and reward (or lack thereof)—the more likely is the employee to consider appraisal as a retrospective process rather than part of an ongoing relationship with the supervisor. Indeed, since some employees have been known to alter their performance for good or ill in even briefer periods than two or three months, such an approach often extends a reward to someone whose performance has recently deteriorated while failing to reward someone whose performance has dramatically improved in recent months.

When appraisal is keyed to an anniversary date, the individual employee is more likely to experience a feeling of personalized attention. Each employee legitimately can feel, at least for a while, that he or she alone is receiving the supervisor's undivided attention.

The Evaluator's Outlook

Then there is the perspective of the evaluator to consider, the outlook of the individual supervisor or manager who must write appraisals and discuss them with anywhere from one or two employees to two or three dozen employees. Although the preference for anniversary-date evaluation seems to dominate among the evaluators, here the preference is not always as evident as it may be with certain other interested parties. Viewing these evaluators for the moment strictly as supervisors and managers who must appraise employees, their view of anniversary-date appraisal versus all-at-once appraisal seems to depend largely on how many employees they have to evaluate. Those evaluators who have small numbers of people to evaluate frequently seem genuinely indifferent to a preference for an approach. After all, doing two or three appraisals over a five week period may not be seen as particularly burdensome, and doing so gets the appraisal process behind them for an entire year. However, the evaluator with 25 employees to appraise within the same five or six weeks is much more likely to favor the opportunity to spread those 25 appraisals out over a full year. (It must be admitted, however, that even some evaluators with larger numbers of people to appraise would just as soon do all of their evaluations at once and thereby get them out of the way for a year at a time. As one head nurse described her feelings, "I'd rather take it on as one massive project to do this month than have it always there, never really finished, demanding my attention again every two or three weeks.")

Interestingly, however, many evaluators who have no strong feelings either way about appraisal timing when viewed from the management perspective nevertheless show a leaning toward anniversary appraisal when considering their own preferences as employees. Surely most appraisers are in turn appraised by higher management. And when the appraisers are appraised as employees, their needs and preferences turn out to be almost indistinguishable from the needs and preferences of rank and file employees.

In the majority of cases the organization's human resource department will display a marked preference for anniversary-date appraisal. This preference is usually founded on the simple view of anniversary-date appraisal as a workload leveler. Ordinarily the human resource department must prepare and distribute appraisal forms, collect results, pursue delinquent evaluations, tabulate scores, and eventually file appraisals in employees' personnel files. Consider the organization of nearly 3,000 employees mentioned earlier. At one point, the human resource department has to ensure that 3,000 forms are prepared and sent to the appropriate evaluators. Further, human resource staff must see that a not inconsiderable number of delinquent appraisals—a whole year's worth of delinquents, one might say—are followed up and collected within a two to three week span. And once appraisal conferences have been completed, within a span of three or four weeks the human resource department must deal with a full year's worth of appraisal filing. Under anniversary-date appraisal, however, the appraisal-related work of the department is distributed evenly throughout the year.

A CLEAR PREFERENCE—AND A CATCH

The foregoing comparison may have made it seem as though there is little or no sound reason for an organization to adopt—or even to continue with—all-at-once appraisal.

It is indeed the case that anniversary-date appraisal holds the edge over all-at-once appraisal from the perspectives of the various people involved in performance appraisal. However, when there is a performance-based merit raise determined by performance appraisal, from a conservative financial perspective the all-at-once appraisal approach has the clear, undeniable advantage of total financial predictability.

Consider again the example of the organization of nearly 3,000 employees that relies on all-at-once appraisal. In late November and early December when all of the scores are tabulated and the score distributions have been determined, various arrays of potential merit increases, each increase amount associated with a particular level of score, can be tested against the amount of money available for merit raises. This is done by computer, and a given array of potential increase amounts can be altered and run as many times as necessary. In this way the merit increases can be established so that they spend all of—but absolutely no more than—the total amount of money that has been identified as the maximum available for merit increases. Thus the all-at-once appraisal approach lends itself to total financial predictability: the organization knows exactly how much its merit increases are going to cost before any raises are granted. It also allows for advance manipulation of the total amount of raise dollars available. The organization surely will have budgeted a particular amount of money, estimated as much as a year earlier, as the amount to be allowed for merit increases. However, since this budgeted amount remains untapped right up to and including the pay period before the annual increase, it can be readjusted at the last moment and a new amount can be distributed with total equity. Depending on where the organization's operating results appear to be leading, the pay increase budget can be boosted to allow for greater raises than originally might have been anticipated or shaved to balance the budget through lower raises than anticipated.

A conservative finance department might fight hard to retain all-at-once appraisal for the sake of retaining the aforementioned financial predictability and hanging onto the ability to adjust the total amount of money available for merit increases. And in these years of continuing financial uncertainty in the delivery of health care services, a chief financial officer can hardly be blamed for wanting to retain the few aspects of control and predictability that still exist. However, there are equally strong countervailing arguments suggesting that employees' pay raises should be far from the first place to look for assistance in balancing the budget.

It is quite true, as the common financial argument contends, that an anniversary-date appraisal approach with associated merit increases does not lend itself to total predictability. There is always the legitimate fear that, having no precise target to work against, appraisers will award merit increases that overspend the budgeted funds as the year progresses. Without reasonable guidance and control it is possible, for example, to arrive at the end of September with three quarters of the year gone and roughly three quarters of the year's merit raises granted but with none of the budgeted money left. This may be considered an extreme example, perhaps, but this is exactly what has happened in a number of organizations.

With proper guidance provided for evaluators it is possible to ensure that the year and the money run out much more closely than three months apart. However, there is no use pretending that the total cost of anniversary-date merit increases will ever be as completely predictable as the total cost of all-at-once merit increases. Again, the all-at-once approach offers total financial predictability; the anniversary date approach, even at its very best, offers something less than complete predictability.

An organization can reduce the chances of dramatically missing its merit increase target under an anniversary-date appraisal system by subdividing the organization's merit budget into a series of departmental budgets. However, this process intensifies the need for management training in how to apply the system, expands training to include instruction on how to properly manipulate the department's merit budget, and leaves the year's merit-pay bottom line subject to as many potential variations as there are departments.

FURTHER FINANCIAL CONSIDERATION

In spite of the financial concerns just related, this chapter presents an argument in favor of anniversary-date appraisal accompanied by a merit increase related to appraisal score. In conjunction with this, it also recommended that organizations that adjust wages once each year, perhaps rolling together a small merit increase with a market adjustment or cost-of-living raise, give serious consideration to clearly separating these two increments. Whether an organization's pay raises are openly referred to as all merit or only partly merit, it remains common practice, ordinarily at the time the increases are given, to "move the scales over" a certain amount to reflect the conditions of the economy and the marketplace.

Consider, for example, that a particular organization might have budgeted 5 percent for increases for the year. It might ordinarily have granted increases that averaged 5 percent, perhaps ranging from 3 percent to about 7 percent. Consider next that it also increased the minimums and maximums of pay grades by 3 percent to reflect conditions in the employment market. Thus, the organization has given an increase that is actually made up of two components: a merit component and a market component. Consider next how the organization can keep its wage scales consistent with the marketplace, yet individualize its appraisal and compensation systems through performance-related merit increases. A likely answer is to be found in the separation of the market and merit components into two distinctly different actions.

Assume that the best available reading of the labor market indicates that an average 3 percent market adjustment would be in order for the coming year. At some other point during the year, pay grades are adjusted by an average 3 percent (although some grades may move more or less than 3 percent depending on certain factors) and most employees receive an across-the-board 3 percent increase. After taking care of adjustments to the labor market, the equivalent of

2 percent of annual payroll would remain available for distribution throughout the year in the form of merit increases.

There are any number of ways of apportioning the 2 percent of payroll that would go into merit increases, but the safest and most equitable way is probably the division of the available amount into smaller departmental amounts as described earlier. In a fair apportionment of money available for merit raises, each department would then have an amount of money equal to 2 percent of its approved personnel budget available for increases for the year. Under the simplest possible form of distribution, merit raises of 0-4 percent or more are possible. (There are numerous possible distribution scenarios that are best left to the compensation specialist. Since merit raises would not occur all at once, but rather throughout the year, the fiscal impact of any specific increase on the current year will be different. For example, a 3 percent increase effective July 1 will have just two-thirds of the fiscal impact on the current year of a 3 percent increase granted April 1. Viewed another way, the April 1 increase costs half again as much of the current year's available increase pool as the July 1 increase costs. Any number of scenarios are possible, but one overriding constraint remains in place—the total amount of money actually paid out in merit increases for the complete budget year cannot total more than the available merit pool, or, in the case of our example, 2 percent of the department's approved personnel budget.)

The organization's compensation specialists can provide information concerning a reasonable range and distribution of possible increases, and supervisors and managers can be trained in the proper application of these guidelines so that the total amount spent on merit increases for the year comes out reasonably close to the total funds available.

Certainly this approach to the distribution of merit pay calls upon supervisors and managers to become far more involved in matters of compensation than may have been the case before for many of them. However, this approach places the critical decisions involving reward for performance exactly where they belong—in the hands of the immediate supervisor. This approach places greatly increased responsibility directly in the hands of the supervisor and encourages the supervisor to accept and fulfill this responsibility. Placed in this position of added responsibility, the supervisor cannot help but grow as a manager.

THE TIMING THAT MATTERS MOST

The first paragraph of this chapter referred to the importance to the evaluated employee of the evaluation's timing relative to the employee's expectations of the process. It is in this sense that timing is everything or can at least seem to be everything. The employee might not be happy overall with the scheduled timing of an appraisal interview. For example, under the all-at-once approach where two or more months can elapse between the writing and the interview, the employee might wish for more immediacy but be fully able to understand why the built-in delay exists. However, if the expected time of the appraisal interview comes and goes and the interview has not occurred, the entire appraisal process is potentially undermined.

The overwhelming majority of employees want feedback on their performance. Whether they consciously realize what they want, whether they can or cannot take suggestions or criticism, whether they actively seek information about how they are doing, most employees want to know where they stand with the organization that employs them. They wish to hear about their performance, even though a great many—including most of those who claim to welcome constructive criticism—do not want to hear anything unfavorable. For the most part they wish to know that they are seen in a favorable light, will probably continue to receive regular pay increases, and are likely to remain relatively secure in their employment.

An employee who knows that an appraisal interview is scheduled to occur within a particular time frame has expectations of feedback on performance. Considering the relative strength of the supervisor-employee relationship (and seldom is this relationship all that it could or should be), these expectations can range from moderate to high. When these expectations are not met because an appraisal interview has not occurred when it was supposed to occur, the appraisal system's credibility suffers and the employee is left with cause for doubt and uncertainty.

The employee who receives no appraisal feedback lacks knowledge of where he or she stands with the organization. This lack may not bother some employees at all; however, it will eventually bother a great many employees in one way or another. Feedback is required to mitigate doubt and uncertainty, and for many people even the certainty of criticism or generally negative feedback is preferable to the unknown state that exists without feedback.

The primary objective of performance appraisal is to maintain or improve performance in the job the employee presently holds. Its secondary objective is to facilitate growth and advancement for the sakes of both the employee and the organization. In serving these objectives, two important questions must be answered for the employee: How am I doing in the eyes of my supervisor? Where do I stand with this organization? If these questions are not answered when the employee has come to expect an answer, the entire performance appraisal process is perceived to have little value for the employee. In this critical respect timing is indeed everything.

7

Face to Face:
The Appraisal Interview

THE PIVOTAL ACTIVITY

From the point of view of the evaluator the appraisal interview is but one step in the appraisal process. Admittedly, it is a large step, one which, along with actually writing the appraisal, is often approached with dread, but it remains a single event in a series of events. However, to the employee, who usually expects the appraisal meeting to occur within a specific period of time, the interview often *is* the appraisal. The employee sees almost none of the activity that occurs before the appraisal interview and often very little of what follows. The employee who says, "My annual review is scheduled for tomorrow," or "I had my appraisal this morning," is usually talking about an appraisal discussion.

If an appraisal discussion did not occur because the manager seemed always a bit too busy and perhaps because "performance was okay—there weren't any real problems, anyway," the employee sees the result as no appraisal, period. Chances are the employee knows nothing of the work that might have gone into creating a written appraisal or the circumstances that allowed the manager to conclude there were no problems. Without the interview, the appraisal never happened.

This chapter presents the essentials of a fair, thorough, and constructive performance appraisal interview. The appraisal interview is sometimes difficult, occasionally unpleasant, and frequently unpredictable. Nevertheless, this kind of interview remains the best means available to learn directly what an employee thinks or feels about important performance-related issues.

Serving Appraisal's Objectives

The performance appraisal interview typically serves two major functions:

1. evaluation and discussion for administrative decisions
2. counseling and development[1]

The administrative decisions referred to include matters of salary changes and consideration of promotions, transfers, and other job status changes. The counseling and development aspect of the interview addresses job performance and its improvement.

Over and above these major functions, however, lie the overall objectives of the performance appraisal process, as articulated in Chapter 1:

1. to maintain or improve performance in the job the employee presently holds
2. to enhance the development of employees so as to:
   • provide the organization with persons capable of accepting greater responsibility
   • aid those employees who seek growth and advancement

Although much current performance appraisal theory would isolate all administrative decisions from issues of counseling and development and would keep the former completely out of the process, doing so is no longer practical. Employees in general have come to strongly associate matters of reward or punishment (as reflected in administrative decisions) with level of performance. To many employees, for example, a promotion or pay raise is the logical reward for good performance. Most employees enter the appraisal interview associating acceptable performance with tangible rewards, or at least with positive strokes and assurances such as the reassurance of a reasonable degree of job security.

In brief, the employee who is about to enter into an appraisal interview usually wants to know:

• What's in this for me?
• How am I doing?
• Where can I go from here?

The appraisal interview, therefore, must not only serve the stated objectives of performance appraisal; it must also fulfill the employee's expectations of the process.

MAKING THE NEGATIVE POSITIVE

The performance appraisal interview need not be approached by the evaluator as a necessary evil. It is helpful to recognize the interview as necessary, but when the evaluator gives in to negative feelings about the process the opportunity for constructive interchange is greatly restricted. When it is apparent that an upcoming evaluation necessarily will involve some negative commentary, the evaluator should be careful not to allow avoidance techniques to come into play, such as postponing the interview repeatedly or rationalizing away the critical elements. Instead, the evaluator should examine his or her attitude toward the upcoming contact and take it as a challenge, asking:

- How well can I do this difficult task?
- What can I learn in the process?

Little is to be gained by the manager who simply goes through the appraisal interview as quickly and painlessly as possible; this evaluator is simply conforming with a general, unimaginative level of expectations and is avoiding potential discomfort. Thorough preparation is by far the most effective means of blunting an initial uneasiness about the appraisal interview, and the repeated experience of many well-prepared appraisal interviews is the best way to get better at the process.

However, the well-prepared evaluator who is not afraid to criticize must also take an additional step and recognize that criticism itself, even compassionate, fully constructive criticism, will not itself generate change. The very best the evaluator can hope to achieve through criticism is to inspire behavioral change. Change must come, self-initiated, from within the individual.

ONE-ON-ONE: THE ACTUAL DISCUSSION

For those who might find it helpful to categorize interviews by type according to their basic purposes, under most circumstances the appraisal discussion is a problem-solving interview. It can at times exhibit characteristics of the information-gathering interview (a type best represented by the more-or-less standard employment selection interview) as the evaluator attempts to learn more about the person being counseled, but by and large the appraisal interview works best if it is simply a two-way discussion of common concerns.

The essentials of an effective performance appraisal interview are discussed below.

The Setting

The need for privacy and freedom from interruptions demanded by an appraisal interview may seem so obvious that it need not be mentioned. An appraisal interview is an intensely personal exchange between manager and employee; no one else need hear what transpires. It is not one of the many items of day-to-day business that can be conducted within the hearing of others. If the evaluator does not have a private office, as many first-line supervisors do not, he or she needs to borrow space in which appraisal discussions can be held in private.

When planning an appraisal interview—and any such interview should always be scheduled at least a few days in advance—the evaluator who has no private office should reserve a conference room, arrange to use a superior's or other manager's private office, or request the use of an interview room in the human resource department.

When scheduling an appraisal interview, it is best to allow 45 minutes to an hour. Some interviews, usually those that are relatively trouble free, may be satisfactorily concluded in less time. However, it is not always possible to predict the nature of any particular performance discussion in advance, so it is best to allow some extra time in case it is needed. If it is known in advance that the meeting will be in part a joint target setting work session (see Chapter 15), sufficient additional time should be allowed.

A performance appraisal interview should be interrupted only for genuine emergencies. The evaluator should respect the employee's time, especially in regard to this topic of extreme importance to the individual, and not attempt to take telephone calls or transact other business during this period. The employee deserves the evaluator's full attention for the entire appraisal interview.

The best setting for the interview is the appraiser's private office or other private work space. A conference table is helpful; it is better to share a work surface at one end of a table than to face each other across a desk, especially when there are documents (the appraisal form and whatever else is involved) to refer to and perhaps work with.

Some evaluators prefer to deliver appraisals over lunch at some place away from the office, especially when evaluating professional or managerial employees. A pleasant lunch out of the office might be a helpful part of the interchange, but it probably should not constitute the entire interview. The parties are always more free to speak out in private, and when more than a couple of documents are involved it is easier to spread them out in a work setting.

Putting the Employee at Ease

The employee enters the appraisal interview generally aware of the meeting's purpose, knowing, or perhaps feeling, that criticism might be forthcoming. The employee might be wary of possible surprises, feeling uptight to some extent, knowing, after all, that he or she is about to be reviewed.

At some level, whether minimally or overwhelmingly, the employee is ever aware that you, the evaluator, are the boss in this relationship, that there is an authority gap between the two of you. No matter how you come across to the employee there will be many times when the person across the corner of the table from you will be automatically on guard simply because you are the boss.

Therefore, it is extremely important for the evaluator to do everything possible to minimize the immediate effects of the authority gap, to level the conversational playing field by leaving the supervisor-subordinate relationship in the background and dealing with the person on a collegial basis as much as possible. A bit of small talk, a few minutes of social chatter on topics of mutual interest, can be a good investment for the time that will follow. Not everyone requires this kind of treatment, but neither are a great many people capable of smoothly getting right down to business when they have a personal stake in the meeting. As evaluator, be calm, straightforward, and genuinely friendly. With most employees your friendly, interested, and supportive behavior will encourage participation in the kind of dialogue that should occur in a productive appraisal interview.

Building Confidence in the Employee

As a natural follow up to helping the employee get comfortably into the discussion, the evaluator should strive to draw the employee into a willingness to discuss all aspects of his or her performance, to talk about personal objectives as they relate to this employment and possibly beyond, and to volunteer points for the discussion.

As the asking of questions or posing of problems begins, the evaluator needs to create a sense of collaboration, quite literally referring to "we," "us," and "ours" in opening up problems and concerns. The evaluator and the employee always have in common the objectives of the department; these objectives are why both parties are there and why they do what they do. If the two parties can come together in the belief that they are working toward common goals in this meeting, they will have a basis for communication even if there happens to be some disagreement along the way.

Getting the Employee to Talk

Although the best performance appraisal discussions are true two-way exchanges, it remains the task of the appraiser to get the discussion going and to control its direction. Much of the advice regularly extended to interviewers of all kinds applies here, especially as concerns the kinds of questions to ask. In asking questions as conversation starters or continuers:

• Avoid questions that can be answered with just "yes" or "no" or in only one or two words. Your aim should be to get the employee to talk; the employee will often say little of substance if you rely on questions that require the person to speak only minimally.

- Ask one clear question at a time. If you ask, for example, "What do you like best about the work and where do you see yourself going?," you are sending conflicting signals and are likely to get incomplete answers.
- Avoid leading questions. In asking leading questions ("You're not really fond of this part of the job, are you?") you are actually answering yourself, or are at least telling the person what you want to hear or what you believe you are going to hear. Every question should be open to an answer; in leading the employee you are denying yourself potentially valuable information.
- Speak directly, using language that acknowledges the employee's education and position. Talk down to no one; neither speak over anyone's head.

The primary objective in asking questions should be to get the employee to talk about himself or herself in relation to the work. For the employee who seems reluctant to speak much or who is slow at opening up conversationally, it is suggested that the evaluator try a few work-related questions such as, for example:

- What are the most important things you do on your job?
- What do you most enjoy doing?
- What do you dislike doing?
- What things do you do that nobody else does?
- How is your performance unique or special in any way?
- If you had more time available to you, what would you do with it?
- When was the last time you tried something different and it worked?
- How do you really feel about working here?[2]

However, for the employee who fails to raise a particular topic that you feel needs to be covered, perhaps failing to touch on, or perhaps even seeming to deliberately avoid, an area of apparent difficulty, it is fair for you to ask: "How do you plan to improve performance on that task?"[3]

Motivating the Employee

Motivating any employee is always far easier said than done. In the last analysis all true motivation is self-motivation, so it is really the task of the evaluator to create the conditions under which the employee is willing to self-motivate. As a result of the appraisal conference the evaluator wants the employee to do one of the following:

- continue doing what he or she has been doing, if results have been fully satisfactory

- perform differently—preferably more satisfactorily—if that is what appears to be needed

Although behavior change is often a goal of the performance appraisal process, it often is necessarily a longer range goal than is properly served by a single appraisal interview. The appraisal interview usually can be considered a success if it has brought manager and employee closer together on common concerns and has helped the employee develop the willingness to work toward improved performance.

TRAPS, PITFALLS, AND OTHER HAZARDS

Personal Problems

Rarely is it possible completely to separate the person off the job from the person on the job. Problems from one part of a person's life have an effect on other parts; personal problems related to an employee's private life cannot help but affect work performance in some ways. People simply differ in the extent to which they are able to keep problems and pressures in one area of life from affecting other areas. Therefore, it is important to recognize that an employee's problems outside of work can and frequently do have adverse effects on work performance.

When the presence of personal problems is indicated the evaluator must be extremely careful to focus strictly on performance, that is, on the results of behavior. Should the employee tell the evaluator of certain personal difficulties or perhaps ask for advice, the evaluator is free, within relatively narrow limits, to refer the employee to others for professional help. However, the evaluator's primary interest must remain the employee's work performance, and the evaluator must deal with what might be described as substandard performance without attempting to infer causes that lie outside of employment.

Needless to say, the individual who leads a troubled personal life is often a troubled or troublesome employee.

Defensiveness

Nobody can prepare the appraisal interviewer in advance for all likely reactions. However, defensiveness is a sufficiently common reaction that the interviewer is well advised to expect it. Often when an individual experiences a threat of punishment, whether direct or implied, there is an immediate shift to defensiveness. When this occurs the chances of constructive learning and problem solving diminish dramatically.

Unless previous attempts at correction of behavior have failed, it is best to leave the possibilities of punishment—lack of pay increase, demotion, termination, or whatever—well in the background. Initially let the possible consequences be evident by implication only. Direct threats do not motivate most employees; rather, threats usually only foster defensiveness and resentment.

With some employees, criticism, even honest and constructive and compassionately delivered, will lead to defensiveness. In this respect a certain amount of defensiveness is to be expected; the evaluator cannot expect to continually back away from delivering deserved criticism simply because of how it might be taken. Be advised, however, that an appraisal discussion can be made doubly difficult by the first recognizable element of criticism that is offered.

Blind Spots

Most people have favored beliefs and opinions that may amount to psychological blind spots. It is difficult to suggest how to recognize such blind spots and tougher still to advise on how to avoid them; we often cannot see them at all in ourselves. However, they are often there in the form of strong opinions and prejudices that prevent us from seeing other people clearly. To recognize blind spots and be able to compensate for them is to improve interpersonal communication ability vastly.

Identification

Regarding employment selection interviewing, it is often claimed that managers tend to duplicate themselves in the hiring process, that many people unconsciously look for their own beliefs, talents, opinions, and attitudes in the people they hire. Similarly, it is not uncommon for evaluators unconsciously to seek characteristics of themselves in the employees they evaluate. That is to say that the employee whose attitudes and opinions most closely resemble those of the manager might turn out to be the employee with the best evaluation score. Since problems of identification relate more to personality (what the person is) than to performance (what the person does), this gives added weight to the need to focus clearly and deliberately on performance.

The Self Example

Be wary or using yourself as an example in dealing with employees. Doing so is at best a weak way to counsel. At worst it is egotistical.

Promises

Do not be maneuvered into making promises that you cannot keep. It is entirely possible, in the enthusiasm of a stimulating and seemingly successful exchange of ideas, to promise an employee something that is not within your power to extend to every employee similarly situated. Making a promise that you are unable to keep can be considerably more damaging than declining to promise anything at all.

In Summary: Some Simple "Do Nots"

The largest part of appraisal interviewing should consist of nondirective interviewing; the interviewer needs to be friendly, patient, and receptive, and must focus on listening. However, the interviewer must listen with restraint, remaining unaffected by fear, anger, or defensiveness.

Above all else do not:

- *argue with the employee.* Arguing is counterproductive. At best it is allowing the employee to control the interview; at worst it is destructive of communication.
- *scold or reprimand the employee.* Any behavior deserving of reprimand should have been so dealt with when it occurred, not at the time of a formal appraisal discussion. Reprimands or admonitions serve only to increase the potential for disagreement.
- *dispense advice.* Corrective instructions—the constructive part of constructive criticism—are appropriate for aspects of performance, but advice beyond specifically job-related instructions is out of order. By inference, advice addresses cause rather than results of behavior. (Many of the least appropriate evaluators' statements in appraisal discussions begin with the likes of: "If I were you," or "When I was in your position."
- *wield your authority.* The employee well knows that you are the boss and that you automatically have the upper hand in this interchange; indeed, you should have put a fair amount of effort into keeping this authority difference from showing. The most positive results can be achieved when the parties can approach the appraisal more like colleagues than like superior and subordinate. Wielding authority destroys the two-way nature of the process, and it also may indicate that the evaluator has run out of convincing ideas and fallen back on the weapon of last resort.

EMPLOYEE PARTICIPATION AND INPUT

As the appraisal interview progresses the evaluator should actively solicit employee input to the process. Doing so, however, means that the evaluator should be prepared to receive and deal with all employee input that may be forthcoming, even challenge and disagreement.

Do not enter the appraisal interview with all of your ideas, opinions, and decisions firmly set in concrete. There is no weakness involved in an evaluator's altering a point or two of evaluation scoring in response to an employee's input. The evaluator cannot know absolutely everything pertinent about the employee's performance, so the evaluator should be open to legitimate challenge. The evaluator needs to recognize that for the most part nobody knows the inner working details of any given job better than the person who does that job every day.

Accepting input does not mean conceding to employee anger or simply handing out the score that someone believes he or she deserves. Accepting input means remaining open to being convinced that there is something important you did not fully account for in your evaluation of the employee. You may or may not be convinced to change a score, but, most importantly, you have encouraged the employee to express an opinion and have provided the opportunity for the employee to note that opinion on the appraisal form if he or she so desires.

The single condition that does the most to stimulate employee input into the appraisal cannot be created at the time of the interview. That condition is the continuing relationship between manager and employee. If that relationship is such that the parties regularly speak freely with each other in the normal day-to-day conduct of business, this will carry over into the formal appraisal setting. If the relationship is healthy and active, the formal appraisal probably will be pleasant and free of challenges.

When Personal Problems Surface

A supervisor or manager is sometimes put in the position of not-especially-willing listener. Occasionally an employee will simply open up and talk. Although a discussion may have begun on some aspect of business, the employee, for whatever reason, begins to relate personal problems and concerns. This occasionally occurs within the context of the appraisal discussion, with personal difficulties sometimes cited as the root causes of certain apparent performance deviations.

Once again, it is extremely important for the evaluator to stay focused on the results of behavior, the visible products of performance. You cannot account for an individual's personal problems or circumstances in such a way that you modify your performance expectations of this person relative to others. You have to insist on adherence to the same standards of performance that are applied to other employees who do the same kinds of work.

The most constructive posture you can take when hearing an employee speak of personal problems is that of a sympathetic listener. Sometimes no more is required than allowing the employee to ventilate in a nonthreatening situation.

If serious personal problems are being made known to you, do not attempt to diagnose the person's difficulties and do not presume to dispense advice. However, you can and should let the employee know about available sources of pertinent information and professional help that he or she can seek confidentially, such as the organization's employee health service or employee assistance program (EAP).

THE INEVITABLE RECORD

Usually no formal record of most of the appraisal interview is needed beyond the standard appraisal form. However, the evaluator will find it helpful to keep a few anecdotal notes about the nature of the appraisal discussion, along with the evaluator's copy of the appraisal, to refer to as necessary between formal appraisals. The anecdotal notes and other backup documentation should certainly include agreed-on goals or objectives arising from the discussion.

It is important that all of the appraisal form be filled out as required, with all dates in place (usually the date the appraisal was written and the date it was discussed) and the signature of the evaluator and any others who are expected to review the evaluation. Once a particular appraisal goes into the employee's personnel file it is the official record. Regardless of what anyone might have to say in the future about the employee's performance during the period of this evaluation, it is invariably the official record that will prevail (see Chapter 17).

For the sake of the record and any possible future disagreements that call a particular appraisal into question, it is essential that the appraisal's written comments be in agreement with the numeric scores given. For example, if a score for attendance indicates average, standard, or satisfactory but is accompanied by a comment like "Needs to improve attendance" or "Needs to pay attention to use of sick time," there is an inconsistency because the score indicates acceptable performance but the comment suggests problems. Unfortunately this kind of inconsistency is fairly common on appraisals generated by weak or chronically lenient evaluators.

The employee should be asked to sign his or her appraisal. It should be stressed that signing does not necessarily indicate that the employee approves the total appraisal or agrees with everything that appears on it; in signing the employee should be acknowledging simply that he or she has reviewed the appraisal and discussed it with the evaluator. It is helpful if the form indicates that the employee's signature is simply in acknowledgment of receipt of the appraisal. There should also be a space for employee comments, and the employee should be encouraged to append any comments or objections to the appraisal.

Should an employee refuse to sign his or her appraisal, which will occasionally be the case, indicate that refusal on the form. If possible, have the refusal to sign repeated and witnessed by another member of management who will so note and initial that refusal on the appraisal form.

THE SELF-APPRAISAL OPTION

Self-appraisal can be helpful, but there are some compelling reasons for making self-appraisal an option rather than a requirement. Some employees will never be comfortable with self-appraisal; they will worry about how the way they see themselves will in turn be seen, and they will attempt to second-guess the evaluator in many respects. Some will feel that if they rate themselves higher than the boss eventually rates them, they will then be seen as holding unrealistic opinions of themselves; some feel that if they rate themselves lower than the boss eventually rates them, they will be seen as lacking confidence in themselves. The extent to which some employees agonize over self-appraisal suggests that it is not for everyone.

In dealing with an employee who is willing to utilize self-appraisal, the evaluator's ground rules are simple and few:

- Provide the employee with the same evaluation instructions that you will use in writing your evaluation of that person.
- Do not look at the employee's self-appraisal before you write your appraisal of the employee. If you do so you establish some harmful biases and you are likely to let issues surface prematurely when they should be allowed to emerge on their own later.
- Be prepared to negotiate genuinely concerning points of difference between your appraisal of the employee and that person's self-appraisal, and be prepared to alter your conclusions as necessary. In accepting the self-appraisal you are merging two legitimate views of the same performance and attempting to reach consensus.

The primary advantage of self-appraisal is its ability to rapidly focus the appraisal interview on the most important points. If, for example, a given appraisal calls for assessment on 12 significant criteria, and the evaluator's assessment and the employee's self-appraisal are close together on all but two criteria, both parties know at once where their subsequent discussion can be focused most productively.

PARTNERS?

A great deal has been said about the need to put evaluator and employee on as nearly equal a footing as possible in the performance appraisal interview, to stress joint problem solving in a collegial atmosphere. However, it takes two people to hold an effective performance discussion, and most organizations are training only one of them.[4]

All evaluators need to be well trained in appraisal techniques. However, in addition to imparting skills this process also adds competence and confidence to the authority and position of the manager and serves to further accentuate the differences between manager and employee.

This suggests that most employees probably need more information about appraisal than they get at new employee orientations or through employee hand-books. One of the most valuable training moves a manager can make is to insti-tute periodic inservice education in performance appraisal for the department's employees. It is only by making employees as comfortable with the appraisal process as possible through knowledge that the manager can have a reasonable chance of making them full partners in discussing their performance.

NOTES

1. H. Kent Baker and Philip I. Morgan, "Two Goals in Every Performance Appraisal," *Personnel Journal*, vol. 63, no. 9 (September 1984) p. 74.

2. Naomi Domer Medearis, "Conformance or Creativity in Performance Evaluation," *AORN Journal*, vol. 14, no. 3 (September 1971) p. 56.

3. William Weitzel, "How to Improve Performance Through Successful Appraisals," *Personnel*, vol. 64, no. 10 (October 1987) p. 23.

4. Geoff Bellman, "Nine Ways to Upgrade Performance Discussions," *Training*, vol. 18, no. 2 (February 1981) p. 37.

8

Completed Is Just Begun

APPRAISAL AS A CONTINUOUS PROCESS

After the performance appraisal interview has taken place, if the completed appraisal form is simply filed away to remain hidden from all human consideration until it is time for the employee's next annual appraisal, the next appraisal will be fully as difficult for both parties as the one just concluded. If the appraisal is treated as though it is simply a snapshot of performance at a point in time, then it has little value as an aid to employee development.

Employee development is a continuing process, and performance improvement is a large part of this process. The cause of employee development is not served by file-it-and-forget-it appraisals. Within true employee development the performance appraisal, if it has never been so utilized previously, can be a beginning; however, the performance appraisal is never an end.

In its support of a continuing process the performance appraisal provides one means of strengthening the manager-employee relationship. It should be stressed that this is only one means; the relationship between manager and employee will not be especially successful if a periodic attempt at appraising performance is all that passes between the two parties. More is required. There needs to be regular contact of both formal and informal nature. That is, there needs to be a genuine, continuing relationship so that appraisal can enhance and support the relationship and so that appraisal can in turn be enhanced and supported by the relationship. Performance appraisal will be least discomforting and most potentially productive when it is an expected and accepted part of a continuing manager-employee relationship.

As noted in the preface to this book, if the relationship between manager and employee is all that it should be, then appraisal will be a mere formality because both parties will know where they stand with each other at all times. Performance appraisal and the manager-employee relationship are inextricably linked; as the strength of one rises or falls, so rises or falls the strength of the other.

WORKING TOGETHER DAY TO DAY

If employees see their day-to-day supervision as generally fair and acceptable, they are more likely to be satisfied with the role of supervision in the appraisal process. This was a conclusion of a number of studies that also found that the more employees felt they participated in the appraisal process, the more likely they were to feel that supervisors were helpful and constructive, that job problems were solved, and that reasonable goals were set.[1]

If the manager has been coaching or counseling a particular employee on a more or less continuing basis, the topics covered in that context will form the best possible framework for appraisal. In simply sliding from the less formal into the more formal, the manager is correctly introducing appraisal as part of an ongoing developmental process.

Performance problems inevitably arise during the day-to-day conduct of business. Likewise, instances of outstanding performance can occur at any time. The time to acknowledge and deal with both outstanding performance and substandard performance is when it occurs; it is not appropriate to wait until appraisal time. Performance feedback delayed is performance feedback that most likely will have little positive effect and may even have a negative effect. Studies have shown that the longer feedback is delayed the less likely it is to motivate behavior and behavioral change.[2]

Informal, day-to-day performance feedback is essential. But formal, once-per-year feedback is essential as well. Informal performance feedback furnished on an ongoing basis provides some definite impetus for change, but the formal evaluation system probably provides the clearest standards and thus represents an important source of feedback and motivational leverage.[3]

Employees want, need, and certainly deserve performance feedback, but frequently they do not seem eager to obtain this feedback via formal performance appraisal. Studies have indicated that employees generally want more frequent and continuous informal appraisal, with informal appraisal being defined as day-to-day or casual feedback that reflects the employee's performance.[4] Therefore we can conclude safely that informal day-to-day working contacts can provide the best possible foundation for formal annual appraisal.

APPRAISING BETWEEN APPRAISALS

It should be apparent by this point that there is a need to make appraisal a year-round way of life in the workplace. The formal evaluation should not be an annual chore for managers or a dreaded judgment day for employees.[5]

What occurs from one formal appraisal to the next need not always be planned or structured as long as it includes appropriate working contact with the employee. However, neither should all employee contact just happen without apparent purpose. A variety of approaches are open to the manager; essentially all of them should be utilized from time to time.

Schedule Interim Performance Conferences

One approach that helps keep performance objectives at the forefront of employees' daily work lives is to schedule regular evaluations throughout the year. At least quarterly, and sometimes even monthly, the manager who rates the employee at the end of the year can review the subordinate's progress toward objectives.[6] There is certainly no prohibition against reviewing performance more often than once per year within your own department, and since these interim previews are not an organizational requirement they need not be as formal as scheduled annual reviews. Neither need they be as paper-generating; you need create nothing for the official personnel file, but rather just utilize anecdotal notes.

These interim appraisal conferences can be extremely useful for performance coaching. The employee and the manager can review the employee's performance relative to goals, objectives, and standards; the supervisor can supply corrective feedback as needed; and the two can jointly develop revised objectives and expectations as needed.

Guiding employees through these interim reviews or coaching sessions and orienting them toward improved performance essentially involves encouraging them to change behavior. Here, in dealing with employee resistance to change of any kind, the manager frequently has three possible approaches available:

* tell the employees what to do
* convince the employees of what they must do
* involve the employees in determining what must be done

The preferred approach, of course, is to involve the employees in determining what is to be done. It is only sometimes necessary to rely solely on convincing employees of what must be done; for example, it may be necessary to have an employee change the way some task is accomplished because of a new regulatory requirement, yet the employee may be sufficiently resistant to need to be sold on the method. Convincing someone to change is always an option. Simply telling the employee—giving an order without explanation or discussion and expecting compliance—should remain the alternative of last resort, utilized rarely, and only when a reasonable effort to convince the employee has failed.

In dealing with potential behavior change it may be necessary initially to convince the employee that there is a performance problem. Once the employee has acknowledged the problem, or has at least acknowledged the likelihood of a problem or the possibility of room for improvement, then the employee can become genuinely involved in the process. Manager and employee then can work together planning for change through the development of goals, objectives, targets, timetables for completion, and such.

Hold Open-Agenda Meetings

Every month or two schedule a time to meet with each employee without any specific agenda items known in advance. This gives the employee the chance to talk privately with the manager about anything he or she wishes to bring into the conversation. One need allocate only 15 or 20 minutes to such a meeting, though the occasional such contact will bring to the surface topics or concerns that demand more time and attention.

The manager should ask the employee a few simple questions intended to offer the opportunity for a work-related conversation of an unthreatening nature. For example:

- How has the job been going since the last time we spoke?
- Do you feel any differently about your work since we last talked about it?
- Have you experienced any problems that you would like to ask me about?
- Is there anything that you believe you need help with?

If any negatives enter into the discussion they should be raised only by the employee. The manager should limit his or her remarks to positive comments as appropriate (these meetings are great opportunities for telling people they are doing well) and to questions, like those above, that stimulate work-related conversation.

The objective of these open-agenda meetings is well met if employees leave with a sense of having had the manager's personal attention in a private conversation. This cannot help but serve to strengthen the manager-employee relationship and reinforce performance appraisal as simply a part of that continuing relationship.

Be Visible and Available as a Manager

The management job is often described as getting things done through people. To get things done through those all-important people—employees—

supervisors should (1) be visible and available, spending most of their time where they are really needed; (2) show concern for their employee's problems; (3) maintain an "open-door" attitude; and (4) rely on immediate feedback to let all of their employees know exactly where they stand.[7]

As a manager you should continually go out of your way to make it easy for your employees to communicate with you. Your visibility and availability will enhance the purpose for which your position exists in the first place: to ensure that your employees' work gets done more efficiently and effectively with you than it would without you. The manager who is continually away from the department or constantly tied up on nondepartmental matters cannot appropriately fulfill basic people-management responsibilities. Even effective delegation involving capable subordinates will not carry full weight without the manager's involvement. The manager is (or should be) the primary support system for each direct reporting employee, and if that system is not accessible the manager-employee relationship begins to break down.

Be seen and be reachable by the employees. Wander around the department. Address problems, issues, and complaints as they arise, and do not forget those quiet, satisfactory performers who never call themselves to your attention through their actions. The visible and available manager will benefit from stronger work relationships with most employees.

Share Positives and Negatives as They Arise

It bears frequent repetition that nothing, whether favorable or unfavorable, should be "saved up" for the formal evaluation. Praise delayed is praise largely relieved of its impact, and the "gotcha!" approach to revealing criticism upon appraisal is practically guaranteed to reduce the chances of correcting the offending performance or behavior.

When you notice an instance of commendable performance, acknowledge this to the employee. If it strikes you as significant, also make yourself a note for your anecdotal file to be reflected in a later appraisal. Should you receive a written commendation concerning an employee, provide a copy to the employee, a copy for your appraisal note file, and perhaps a copy for the permanent personnel file if such is your organization's practice. You might also consider posting many such commendations in the department for all to see; frequently praise for one of your staff reflects positively on the entire group.

Whether dealing with aspects of performance or behavior problems related to policy adherence, address matters as they arise within the context of a continuing relationship with the employee.

Keep Anecdotal Notes Lean and Current

As cautioned throughout this book, put nothing on paper that you could not successfully defend or reasonably prove if it were to become public. In maintaining anecdotal note files concerning an employee:

- Regularly purge used items (those that have been incorporated into a formal appraisal).
- Discard notes that are no longer relevant. If, for example, you made an earlier note concerning a problem that appeared to be developing, but never really materialized or was corrected early, get rid of it.
- If you have talked with the employee about an apparent problem, indicate in your note that you have spoken with the person and note the person's response or reaction (taking care to avoid subjective commentary).
- Keep notes concerning targets or objectives to the extent that you may need them from one appraisal to the next.

As also cautioned elsewhere, never create a note (or any business-related document whatsoever, regardless of how informal it may be) without dating the page.

THE MANAGER AS A KEY FACTOR

The immediate supervisor is always a key determinant of whether a given employee will "make it" over the long run. The manager's general style and approach can have a great deal to do with whether the employee succeeds or fails. However, far too many managers have been quick to write off so-called substandard or unsatisfactory employees without examining their own behavior. Many managers are not prepared to recognize that some employees would not fail unless the manager had failed the employee in some way.

It is up to the manager to monitor employee performance and take all reasonable steps to ensure that it remains acceptable. This is critical for a manager; studies have shown that the key behavior that separates excellent from less effective managers is performance monitoring, or the constant gathering and evaluating of performance information.[8]

The variables of individual employee ability and motivation go only so far. Other determinants, which can be described as opportunity or system variables, can sometimes account for as much as 90 percent of the variance in work performance. The common opportunity or system variables include: leadership practices, appraisal frequency, and praise and reward practices.[9]

There is indeed much more than individual motivation and ability involved in employee success. Managers also must do their best to ensure that employees succeed, and doing so includes treating performance appraisal as a never-ending process.

NOTES

1. Dorothy L. Lowell Goode, "Higher Education Managers' Perceptions of the Performance Appraisal Interview," *Personnel Administrator*, vol. 29, no. 10 (October 1984) p. 88.

2. Sanford L. Bordman and Gerald Melnick, "Keeping Productivity Ratings Timely," *Personnel Journal*, vol. 69, no. 3 (March 1990) p. 50.

3. *Ibid.*

4. Jim Laumeyer and Tim Beebe, "Employees and Their Appraisal," *Personnel Administrator*, vol. 33, no. 12 (December 1988) p. 76-77.

5. Robert J. Sahl, "Design Effective Performance Appraisals," *Personnel Journal*, vol. 69, no. 10 (October 1990) p. 53.

6. *Ibid*, pp. 54 & 56.

7. Charles R. McConnell, "The Visible Supervisor," *The Health Care Supervisor*, vol. 1, no. 2 (January 1983) p. 41.

8. Craig Eric Schneier, Arthur Geis, and Joseph A. Wert, "Performance Appraisals: No Appointment Needed," *Personnel Journal*, vol. 66, no. 1 (November 1987) p. 80.

9. David A. Waldman and Ron S. Kenett, "Improve Performance by Appraisal," *HR Magazine*, vol. 35, no. 7 (July 1990) p. 67.

Part III
The Mechanism:
Designing an Integrated
Appraisal System

9

Appraisal: The Core of an Integrated System*

A FACT OF ORGANIZATIONAL LIFE

While not often the subject of a great deal of praise, performance appraisal is a generally accepted fact of organizational life. Many managers, perhaps the vast majority, would probably concede to the need for some form of performance appraisal—some means of providing assessment and feedback concerning employee performance—though many also might voice a preference for appraisal approaches other than the ones they happen to be using. However, for its adherents and for those who simply tolerate its existence, performance appraisal remains a target for continuing criticism.

NO ISOLATED ACTIVITY

The place of performance appraisal in the modern health care organization has solidified during recent years. In the not-too-distant past appraisal was largely an option of management. It existed because of the basic belief in the need to supply such assessment and feedback in order to maintain or improve employee performance. Appraisal had found its place earlier in the general industrial and business setting, and it began to spread through other sectors of the economy, not because of any outside requirements, but because it was becoming a more widely accepted management technique.

Now, however, performance appraisal in the majority of health care organizations is more than a management option and a simple, visible sign of management concern. Accreditation and regulatory organizations now require the presence of an active appraisal system. Representatives of accreditation and regulatory organizations look for such systems during periodic facility surveys.

Beyond looking for the mere existence of an appraisal system, some survey-

---

*Significant portions of this chapter first appeared in Charles R. McConnell, "An Integrated View of Performance Appraisal," *The Health Care Supervisor,* vol. 5, no. 4 (July, 1987) pp. 61–78.

ing agencies have gone to the extent of specifying the kind of appraisal process that should be used. For example, the Joint Commission on Accreditation of Healthcare Organizations (the Joint Commission) specifies in its current standards that nurses be evaluated using criteria-based performance appraisal instead of other possible methods of appraisal.[1]

A system of performance appraisal has also become a virtual necessity in complying with the laws governing employment and in dealing with employee advocacy agencies such as a state's division of human rights and the federal Equal Employment Opportunity Commission (EEOC). When an advocacy agency acts on the complaint of an employee who has been laid off or otherwise terminated, or an employee subjected to any other disciplinary action in connection with performance, the organization is invariably called on to produce documentation concerning the employee's performance before the action was taken. The advocacy agency will attempt to determine whether the employee was given the opportunity to correct the alleged performance problems. If formal documentation—particularly performance appraisals—is not available to show that the employee was consulted about the problems, the employee is likely to receive the benefit of the doubt. It is helpful to remember that advocacy agencies frequently fall back on one simple rule: If something was not documented, it is assumed not to have occurred.

For the foregoing and many other reasons, it is necessary to have a working performance appraisal system in place. Because appraisal has, in just a few years, made the transition from option to requirement, a given appraisal system must do everything it is called upon to do. Because appraisal can no longer be avoided, and because its results are continually coming under close scrutiny, it has become necessary to bring appraisal up to date and improve the way it is accomplished.

This is the juncture at which many health care organizations find themselves. They have appraisal systems, have perhaps had them for years, but they need to make these systems better. They need to make certain that these systems are nondiscriminatory and that the processes satisfy all applicable regulations and standards. At the same time organizations also need to ensure that their systems continue to fulfill the basic performance improvement and employee development objectives of performance appraisal.

Reacting to today's emphasis on performance appraisal, many organizations have undertaken sincere efforts to improve the way they evaluate employee performance. Many such organizations have quickly learned, however, that it is difficult, if not impossible, to improve performance appraisal by focusing on performance appraisal alone. A variety of known problems are experienced with performance appraisal, some related to system structure and administration, some related to the attitudes of evaluators and employees, and some related to inconsistency of system application. However, common problems of performance appraisal are dealt with elsewhere throughout this book. This chapter deals with one major but seldom addressed problem area: the difficulties encountered because appraisal is not an isolated process but is rather only one of a number of interdependent processes, none of which can be substantially altered without affecting the others. In short, appraisal presents difficulties because of its position in the larger network of systems in which it must function.

It is necessary to examine performance appraisal in its proper position relative to all other related systems and subsystems. It must be recognized that performance appraisal today does not stand alone as a process in its own right, and that in the future it will depend even more on the structure and function of related activities. Performance appraisal currently may be described as lying near the heart of a collection of interrelated systems. How thorough an appraisal system is and how well it works in manager-employee relationships depends a great deal on that which surrounds it and feeds into it and that which follows it. The result of examining appraisal in this new light should be a systems approach to the evolution of performance appraisal as an ever-improving process of maximum possible value to organization and employee alike.

THE INTEGRATED VIEW

An effective current performance appraisal begins with a sound job description. The job description itself starts elsewhere, however, and contrary to the way many organizations approach job descriptions, a single job description is not appropriate for all major uses to which such a document may be put. Many organizations create a single job description for each job and proceed to use this as source information for performing a job evaluation to determine the position's grade and eventually its salary; creating recruitment advertising and the employment specifications that recruiters will follow in filling the position; providing a list of tasks and responsibilities to serve as performance appraisal criteria; and other purposes, foremost among which is providing a basis for employee instruction and training. These and other uses are all different from one another; each emphasizes some information that the others do not use. Some use a greater or lesser number of pieces of information than the others, some use the same information in different ways, and no single application of the job description utilizes all the information available. Thus, in attempting to make a single document serve a number of varied purposes a job description has been created that does not fully lend itself to any one of those purposes. However, designating clear criteria for a performance appraisal requires a job description that is written in a particular way and ideally requires an additional step between job description and performance appraisal.

Look at Figure 9–1 and consider the position of the actual performance appraisal relative to the activities that feed into it and those that follow the appraisal after it is put on paper.

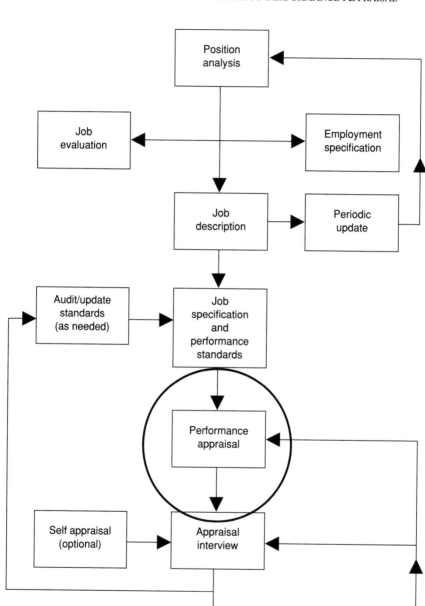

Figure 9–1 Performance Appraisal within an Integrated System

A great many appraisal problems arise because of attempts to extract specific evaluation criteria for each employee from a job description that is either written too generally in order to cover the jobs of a number of people whose work may be partially the same, or, although written specifically for the given job, is a cumbersome multipurpose document created to serve a variety of purposes noted earlier (salary determination, recruitment and advertising, appraisal criteria, training, etc.).

One possible way to overcome some of these problems partially is to choose the second type of job description; that is, have an all-encompassing, general-purpose job description specifically written for each distinctly identified job in the organization. In the extreme, however, this can lead to a proliferation of job descriptions. For example, one organization of slightly more than 2,000 employees was able to count nearly 500 job descriptions in its central files. Among these, approximately 15 job descriptions were identified as variations on the job of medical secretary, utilized in 15 different areas. While these 15 job descriptions were similar for two-thirds or more of their content, the differences among them were sufficient to inspire the need for separate job descriptions, so that each medical secretary in the organization could be evaluated in a way that properly accounted for the unique aspects of each secretarial position.

The major questions addressed before the establishment of the subsystem interrelationships of Figure 9–1 were: How can the job description be cleaned up to provide specific pertinent input to the performance appraisal process? At the same time, how can other legitimate needs for job description information be served as well? How can the criteria essential for performance appraisal be provided in a way that allows for constant improvement in the way in which performance is measured?

Position Analysis

From recognizing the legitimate multiple uses for basic information about a job, it is but one brief step to concluding that information for a number of single-purpose applications could be extracted from one source. That one source, as identified in Figure 9–1, may be referred to as the position analysis. The position analysis would include all information about a given position that conceivably could be needed for any purpose within the organization. The creation of the position analysis and the identification of all the information it should include ordinarily would be a collaborative effort involving human resource practitioners and a number of working managers. Although the designation of position analysis may be new to some, in many cases the document itself would not be new; it would simply be the multipurpose, all-encompassing document that many now call the job description.

Using a thorough position analysis as a base of information, at least three major processes would follow. Certain information would be extracted for the process of job evaluation so that a salary grade might be determined. Other information, different in some respects from that already applied in job evaluation, would apply to the creation of basic employment specifications for the job. Finally, more information, again different from that extracted for the other uses, would go into the creation of a generic job description for the particular title and grade in question.

As mentioned above, the term "generic" is significant. The form of job description recommended here is one that would allow that document to apply equally to all variations internal to the same grade and title position. For example, applying this concept of job description there would be *one* job description for medical secretary, rather than 15 job descriptions each capturing the requirements unique to each department employing medical secretaries. Following this approach the organization having nearly 500 job descriptions would be able to reduce that number to, perhaps, 150. Doing so, however, would lead many to ask immediately: Where do we then obtain the criteria for evaluating the people who work in each specific medical secretarial position? This leads to the component of Figure 9–1 identified as job specification and performance standards.

Job Specification

As the names suggest, job specification and performance standards consist of two distinctly different but obviously related kinds of information. This component may exist initially as a job specification only, with no performance standards appearing as part of it. In fact, this document (which may be referred to for the time being simply as the "job spec") is extremely useful in performance appraisal even if it is introduced when no performance standards yet exist. The specifications portion of the job spec for a particular person's position springs directly from the job description. Thus, in the case of the medical secretary, one generic job description made up of reasonably general statements gives rise to perhaps 15 different job specs. Each job spec is made up of a number of brief descriptions of duties and responsibilities, with each description a specific statement that springs from one of the more general statements in the job description.

Having arrived at the point of employing job specs, even without yet considering the task of acquiring performance standards, the organization will have solved a number of problems. First, the proliferation of job descriptions will have been reversed and their numbers reduced to manageable levels. Second, the job descriptions, being more generic in nature than they previously were (one could perhaps more appropriately call them descriptions of job families) would need to be updated far less often than before. Changes of duties of individuals in specific positions need to be made in the one-page job spec only. Third, and by far most important, the organization will have solved the problem with vertical scale in performance appraisals by moving entirely away from an evaluation based on personality characteristics or individual character traits. Since the job spec consists of a series of concise statements of duties and responsibilities, this will ensure that each person will be appraised solely on the results of his or her performance. Thus a true criteria-based appraisal will have been established. Of course, the problem of horizontal scale in performance appraisals will remain (for example, the half-dozen or so subjectively assessed levels of performance) but once this stage is reached and criteria-based appraisal is operational in a minimal sense, the judgmental difficulties presented by the horizontal scale can be decreased gradually while the system functions.

All of the foregoing information in this chapter should serve to emphasize that performance appraisal based on the true requirements of the job cannot be established without the appropriate foundation in place. To make clear under-standable appraisal criteria available it is necessary to have clear job descriptions and perhaps even detailed job specs. To arrive at clear job descriptions it is necessary to have some means, such as the position analysis, of gathering and assembling job information. Although these multipurpose pre-appraisal steps need not have occurred exactly as described herein (there could, for example, be an entirely different but fully workable way of gathering job information other than using the position analysis) nevertheless something must be there to form the foundation of performance appraisal.

Appraisal, then, is found near the center of an integrated system. It matters little whether appraisal is actually seen as interrelated with other subsystems. The fact remains that there are mechanisms that must be in place to feed into and otherwise support appraisal before it happens, and certain steps that must follow appraisal so that appraisal will have served its intended purposes.

After the Written Appraisal

The first and most essential follow up to the written appraisal is, of course, the appraisal interview. Above all, the appraisal interview should take place as required by most appraisal systems. Since many managers are not completely comfortable with performance appraisal, and especially are not comfortable with appraisal interviews, in the crush of daily business there may be a tendency to skip appraisal interviews, especially for employees who seem to be "doing okay, anyway." But even employees who are "doing okay" in the eyes of the evaluator need to be told that periodically. Recall that one of the primary objec-tives of performance appraisal is to improve or maintain performance in the job the employee now holds.

Self-appraisal is a helpful supplement to some performance appraisal approaches and thus should be considered a useful element of the overall performance appraisal system. If properly approached, self-appraisal can be extremely useful for employees at most organizational levels. However, self-appraisal should probably remain optional.

Joint target setting can also be an extremely helpful process to incorporate into the appraisal system, particularly as applied with professional, technical, and managerial employees—those people who exercise a fair amount of judgment in their work, enjoy a degree of self-direction, and are in a position to formulate and articulate objectives oriented toward the improvement of their performance.

Follow-up appraisal, or interim appraisal, occurring as part of monitoring against objectives, or perhaps arising out of the need to work on particular performance problems, provides a means of closing the loop on the performance appraisal cycle. It ensures that the individual appraisal need not become simply a dead document that is filed and never seen again until a year later, when the evaluator seeks to recall how he or she rated an employee last year.

Thus, performance appraisal falls into place as a system or technique that is tied inevitably to other management systems or techniques, or, if one wishes to see it as such, an integrated subsystem of a total system. The subsystem view is a practical view, because appraisal cannot be dealt with in a vacuum; it must be treated as a piece of a larger whole. One subsystem cannot be altered dramatically without causing change in others; to effect significant change in one subsystem the other subsystems must be adjusted deliberately as well.

TOGETHER: WORKING SYSTEM AND LONG-RANGE UNDERTAKING

It could require a great deal of effort and several years, not to mention a considerable amount of cost, for management to establish and begin operating a full blown, criteria-based performance appraisal system complete with performance standards. However, without a great deal of expense and in a relatively short time—depending on the initial effort expended, perhaps six months to a year—it is possible to put into place a working system of performance appraisal that eliminates the vertical scale problems associated with personality evaluation and makes it possible for performance standards, the truly costly and time-consuming part of the process, to be added gradually. Thus, it is possible to establish criteria-based appraisal that can be put to good practical use while chipping away at the lengthy task of providing standards that will alleviate incrementally much of the horizontal scale problem presented by subjective relative ratings.

Creating the Position Analysis

The first step is the creation of the position analysis. This is accomplished most effectively by a working committee of interested persons that hammers out a draft, or, more likely, a series of drafts eventually resulting in a relatively detailed form that can be used to capture all pertinent information about a new or restructured position. This committee should consist of human resource professionals who are responsible for recruitment, job evaluation, and perhaps training, working with a number of active evaluators. These active evaluators probably will be managers who have a considerable number of employees to appraise and whose departments include most of the organization's more heavily populated position titles. (Design and implementation of the position analysis are detailed in Chapter 10.)

Developing Job Evaluation Criteria

Once the position analysis mechanism is in place, the analysis of each new or restructured position will lead to the creation of a set of job evaluation criteria to be used for the establishment of a pay grade, a set of employment specifications to be used for recruiting, perhaps an outline that will serve as a guide for employee orientation and training, and a generic job description that will serve as the job description of record for anything from a single unique position to dozens of positions that are similar in grade and title.

For each job description, one or a number of job specs are then created. The job spec, essentially a listing of the specific duties and responsibilities against which each employee will be evaluated, need be only a single page document on which each activity is expressed in the most concise way possible. It is important to note, however, that each specifically identified activity should relate back to a more general statement in the overall job description. This arrangement has the effect of subdividing some of the information in what formerly may have been a single job description of considerable length.

Consider again the example of the position of medical secretary. Once there might have been 15 multipage job descriptions, of which 75 percent or more of the contents were similar. Each would have contained the unique aspects of each different medical secretarial position. Whenever an evaluation had to be performed, it would have been necessary to extract carefully everything that was needed in the way of criteria, in many instances choosing among activities as they applied to an individual position. It would also have been necessary, were the organization dedicated to keeping its job descriptions up to date, to alter some or all of these multipage job descriptions whenever something changed in one or two specific positions. However, using the separate, simplified job spec, a change in one or two duties of one medical secretary would be reflected by some simple changes in one job spec, while the generic job description would remain in place as written. Only in the rare instance when a change was of sufficient magnitude to necessitate reevaluation and perhaps breaking out a particular job as a new position in its own right would it be necessary to go back to working with the generic job description.

The job spec document should be laid out so that the duties and responsibilities can be transferred directly to the performance appraisal form in order of descending importance. Although the performance standards portion of the job spec would not yet exist, the mechanism would nevertheless lend itself to any appraisal approach that uses relative judgmental ratings ranging from an expression of unsatisfactory to an indication of perfect or near perfect.

As long as job specs are kept up to date and generic job descriptions are updated as may be required occasionally, the basis of an appraisal system that can only become stronger with the passage of time is in place; that is, it will become stronger as long as the creation of performance standards is conscientiously pursued.

At this point there is nothing wrong with committing the system to operate with subjective relative ratings for an indefinite period of time; after all, most systems have been operating using such ratings for years. It is suggested, however, that consideration be given to the number of relative ratings used. The more ratings there are, the more the individual evaluator must attempt to subdivide his or her judgment. With more ratings there will be additional natural inconsistencies among evaluators. An example cited earlier involved a system that employed six ratings. There are problems that regularly develop with such a scale, because this even number results in the "standard" being in the third position and actually below the center of the scale. Many evaluators are inclined to regard standard, or "average" (incorrectly applied) as most logically at the center of a scale. Therefore, it is suggested that any system utilize no more than five relative ratings with the description of generally expected performance in the middle of the scale.

Providing Performance Standards

The provision of performance standards can become extremely time consuming, costly, and difficult, especially for people who are unfamiliar with work measurement and the setting of objective performance targets. Performance targets mean just that: quantified targets and objective measures of output. These ideally take the form of a range consisting of a designated target and an acceptable amount of variation about that target.

Ideally, performance standards must relate to concrete criteria, things that can be measured or counted objectively. Many common standards involve an expressed relationship between quantity and time. A standard might be expressed in terms of tests or procedures per hour or perhaps per day, or some similar relationship. A billing clerk might have a target of so many bills per hour. An admitting representative might have a target of so many admissions per shift. A messenger or courier might be measured according to a standard of a certain number of completed trips per shift. A worker in central sterile supply might be measured by a standard of so many packs per hour.

In addition to quantity and time, other factors commonly employed to define performance standards are cost and quality. Generally, most effective and usable performance standards will consist of an expressed relationship between at least two of the four factors of quantity, time, cost, and quality.

The provision of performance standards is addressed in greater detail in Chapter 12.

The creation of performance standards can be a long-range part of an overall performance appraisal system undertaking. However, it cannot be expressed too strongly that the system as outlined and put in place before standards are even attempted is a performance appraisal approach that is at least as workable as what probably existed before. It takes time to develop standards, and to delay a comprehensive appraisal system until standards are fully available could push implementation years into the future.

Other Elements of Performance Appraisal

The steps in Figure 9–1 appearing beyond the written appraisal are all either essential or highly desirable elements of an integrated appraisal system. All of the available good advice concerning these particular activities certainly applies in this approach to appraisal. As mentioned earlier, the appraisal interview is a must, and in most instances it should be a wide-ranging, problem-solving conference with equal participation by both manager and employee. Even in the desirable extreme in which the interview becomes no more than a pleasant formality, it should nevertheless take place.

Many performance appraisal systems allow for the use of employee self-appraisal; the self-appraisal is strongly recommended as part of this integrated approach, at least for the majority of technical, professional, and managerial employees. The self-appraisal is best left optional; it will make some employees uneasy, and they will try to second guess the manager and imagine all types of negative repercussions for rating themselves lower or higher than the manager might rate them.

Peer group appraisal also has a place in this integrated approach, but only if it also remains optional and a few employees agree to participate in appraising each other within the context of a small peer group.

Also appropriate to many technical, professional, and managerial employees is the process of joint target setting and similar variations on management by objectives (MBO), in which manager and employee work together to establish a small set of reasonable improvement targets that are largely suggested by the employee. This process works best with employees who are performing at least at standard in job functions (that is, employees who are not exhibiting performance problems). Joint target setting is oriented primarily toward stimulating individual growth and development and is also extremely helpful in ensuring that active follow up becomes a real part of performance appraisal.

A DYNAMIC PROCESS

A performance appraisal should never be regarded as a fixed mechanism. Rather, it is far more convenient to think of appraisal as a dynamic process that takes place within a dynamic, integrated system. It would, of course, be extremely desirable for the organization to be able to establish complete criteria-based and standards-based appraisal in one massive implementation. This may be possible in organizations that have the means for creating performance standards already in place, or in organizations that are able to spend significant amounts of money with one of the few consulting organizations that have invested hundreds of thousands of dollars in the development of job specifications and standards.

The entire process of developing and implementing a fully integrated approach to performance appraisal can be pursued internally by the organization. In addition to the desire and determination to do so, the only major resource is time—first, a few months to establish the position analysis and create job descriptions and job specifications, and later, many more months, stretching out to perhaps three to five years, to create performance standards that apply to the majority of the job duties on each job specification. In this way the organization can achieve an integrated performance appraisal process that works while it grows.

NOTE

1. *Accreditation Manual for Hospitals*, Joint Commission on Accreditation of Healthcare Organizations, NC 2.4.1 and 2.4.1.1., Nursing Care, p. 134.

10

The Position Analysis:
Multipurpose Foundation*

BEGINNING AT THE BEGINNING

Performance appraisal is dealt with only tangentially in this chapter. However, this chapter is concerned with the establishment of the foundation on which a totally integrated approach to the appraisal of employee performance can be built. The structure itself cannot stand—just as a physical structure cannot stand, at least not for very long—unless a reliable foundation is provided.

In the preceding chapter, performance appraisal was described as an activity or system residing near the center of a collection of interrelated systems. To put the description another way, performance appraisal is but one of a number of interdependent subsystems that together make up an integrated system.

In these days of continued movement into the arena of criteria-based performance appraisal, we are coming to recognize that two related sets of information are necessary if we are to accomplish performance appraisal consistently, constructively, and professionally. These two sets of information are performance criteria and performance standards.

Performance criteria are the tasks, conditions, or requirements against which an individual's performance is assessed. Performance standards are the measures by which performance criteria are judged; standards provide the yardstick against which to measure their related criteria. In the simplest possible terms: the criteria tell us *what* and the standards tell us *how much*.

Performance criteria ordinarily come from job descriptions. Fundamental to the concept of criteria-based performance appraisal is the belief that an employee should be evaluated not on the basis of who he or she is (as in the older, personality-based approaches) but rather should be evaluated on the basis of what he or she does. Thus it comes as no surprise that performance criteria come from that which is usually the only available source of task information about a particular job—the job description. To appraise appropriately, we need evalua-

*This chapter is adapted from Charles R. McConnell, "The Position Analysis: Single Source for Multiple Applications," *The Health Care Supervisor*, vol. 6, no. 4 (July 1988) pp. 72–84.

tion criteria; to establish appropriate criteria, we need thorough, reliable job descriptions; to establish reasonable job descriptions, we need good sources of job information.

Few who actively evaluate employee performance would deny that an effective performance appraisal begins with a sound job description. However, we find a considerable divergence regarding what is or is not an effective job description, where such an instrument comes from, and what uses besides performance appraisal it is to serve.

Managers in a majority of health care organizations regard the job description as an original document; that is, the writing of a job description is the creation of first-level documentation, working largely from conceptual knowledge about the job rather than from any pre-existing document. Also, job descriptions in most health care organizations have been called on to serve purposes other than performance appraisal. A single job description may be used, for example, to:

- indicate the boundaries between areas of responsibility, designating who can—and thus who cannot—do certain kinds of work
- serve as a guide for the organization's employment function, so that job postings and advertisements may be placed and applicants may be told about job qualifications, tasks, and responsibilities
- provide sufficient information about a job so that it may be thoroughly evaluated and placed in an appropriate pay grade
- provide a basis for orienting and training new employees
- provide a record of the division of labor and the apportionment of task responsibility in a given work unit

Job descriptions that reasonably meet all of the foregoing needs ordinarily have one characteristic in common—they include far more information than is required in any of a job description's single uses. To properly serve criteria-based performance appraisal, a job description should be a concise recounting of major job responsibilities in priority order, and, most importantly, it should delineate a particular job in specific detail, reflecting how that job differs from all other similar jobs. However, a significant problem is encountered with this lean, specifically targeted job description: for the most part, it does not apply to most of the common job description uses cited above. Thus the heart of the problem of job descriptions relative to criteria-based performance appraisal is that job descriptions have become lengthy and complex to meet a variety of perceived needs, and in the process they have tended to become sufficiently general to allow for variations from job to similar job. Worse still, a virtual paperwork jungle has grown in which job descriptions are subjected to near duplication over and over again to provide the specific detailed task information required for performance appraisal.

Another level of documentation may be needed in the process of collecting job information and developing the performance criteria against which an employee is evaluated. Working backward from the writing of a performance appraisal, in an ideal situation the manager could encounter:

- a job specification—a simple rendering of an individual's tasks and responsibilities, listed in order of importance or according to percentage of time consumed, comprising the bulk of the individual job (This will, or should eventually, exist in conjunction with a number of performance standards.)
- a job description, which might be more appropriately described as a description of a job family because it would ordinarily provide the descriptive basis for multiple positions (For example, there may be a description of a job family titled Food Service Worker that encompasses, by way of a general description, five or six somewhat different specific food service worker positions that have a great deal in common including pay grade and organizational reporting relationship.)
- a position analysis—a document created to serve all of the previously cited purposes of a job description, doing so in a way that provides all of the data needed about a particular job for all legitimate uses

In what we are calling the position analysis, many might recognize what they now call their job description. It is probably lengthy, perhaps running to several pages. It probably contains more information than is needed for employment purposes, for job evaluation, for employee orientation, or for any other single purpose. And to make it applicable to criteria-based performance appraisal in any meaningful way most of it is probably duplicated repeatedly in attempts to describe different jobs in sufficient detail to facilitate criteria-based appraisal.

THE COMPREHENSIVE SOURCE

After recognizing a number of legitimate uses for basic information about a particular job, it is then reasonable to conclude that information for several varied applications could be taken from a single source. That single source is the position analysis. The position analysis is the first block laid in the foundation of a totally integrated approach to performance appraisal (see Figure 10–1).

The following pages present the information that might be collected in a typical position analysis for a medium sized hospital. The following represents the developmental efforts of an actual group of managers implementing a position analysis instrument that is now in active use. Another organization's individual needs and preferences may be somewhat different. Although there may be subtle and perhaps not so subtle differences in approach from one organization to another, the information presented herein should come fairly close to being rep-

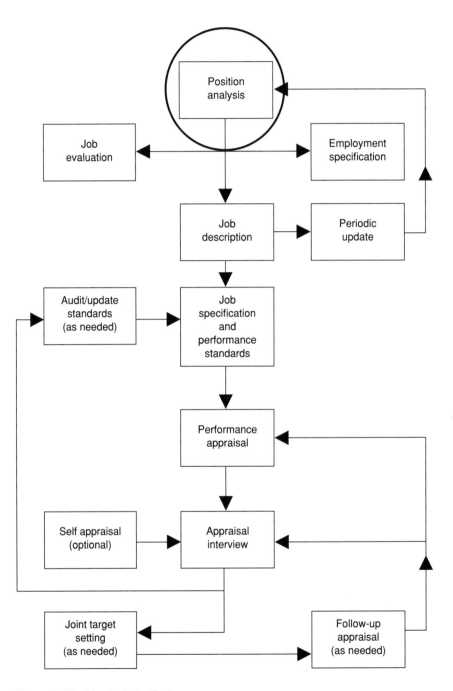

Figure 10–1 Position Analysis: The Source

resentative of the information that any given management group might want to gather concerning the jobs in the organization.

The development of the position analysis is best approached as a collaborative effort. Coordinated by the human resource department, the position analysis development group should include: those human resource professionals responsible for employment, job evaluation, and the publication of job descriptions; at least one manager responsible for training and development; and a number of first-line supervisors and middle managers who have two characteristics in common—they are all required to write job descriptions, and they are all required to appraise employee performance. A working group of ten to twelve persons will not be too large. Given the pressures and unanticipated demands that most such persons are subject to, active membership of ten to twelve will provide reasonable assurance that seven or eight will attend at most working meetings.

The approach consists of developing a draft position analysis, or, more appropriately, a series of drafts with each in turn subjected to detailed critique. After going through several drafts, and once understood and approved by managers who are not directly involved in the creation process, the result will be a data collection instrument that will elicit all job information necessary for all of the organization's normal uses. (A suggested outline of the position analysis development process will be presented later in this chapter.)

What the specific position analysis looks like on paper is not immediately important. As in the process of creating any properly developed form, once the specific contents are decided on, then the physical arrangement of the document can follow. The specific working document resulting from the process described in this chapter appears as Exhibit 10–1.

SAMPLE POSITION ANALYSIS CONTENTS

Heading Information

- *Position title.* If the position under consideration is an existing position undergoing review, the current title as appearing in the organization's job title listings should be entered here. If the analysis concerns a proposed position, the position title should be left blank.
- *Title of supervisor, manager, or chief of service.* Here should appear the official title, as appearing in the organization's job title listings, of the person to whom an employee in the position under consideration would report.
- *Department and cost center number.* The instructions should call for both the name and the cost center number (accounting designation) of the unit or department to which the position belongs.

Exhibit 10–1 Position Analysis Questionnaire

Position Title _____

Title of Supervisor/Manager/Chief of Service_____

Department (Cost Center) _____

Please Check: ( ) New Position   ( ) Position Reevaluation

Proposed Position Title _____

PART I: POSITION OBJECTIVES, ACTIVITIES, RESPONSIBILITIES

A. Position Objectives: State briefly the principal purpose or objectives of the position.

B. List briefly, in order of importance, the activities performed by this position. Start each statement with an active verb that best describes the activity.

Description of Activities	*Frequency (daily, monthly, etc.)*

Suggested Active Verbs

Administer	Calculate	Distribute	Monitor
Allocate	Check	Establish	Operate
Analyze	Code	Estimate	Originate
Appraise	Collect	File	Post
Audit	Compare	Formulate	Record
Authorize	Compile	Initiate	Review
Budget	Compute	Instruct	Schedule
Build	Develop	Interview	Supervise

Exhibit 10-1 continued

C. Describe the contacts a person in this position would have.

In-house contacts:

Outside contacts:

D. Describe the degree, impact, and correctability of errors made on this job.

PART II:

A. Preparation and Training:
What would be the minimum level of knowledge required to qualify for this position? (Check one)

_____ Basic knowledge of arithmetic, English, and grammar; the ability to follow simple instructions where interpretation is not required.

_____ High school diploma or equivalent.

_____ High school diploma or equivalent plus an additional one year of special training (or equivalent one to three years of practical trade training).

_____ Two year college degree or equivalent; completion of an accredited apprenticeship program.

_____ Four year college degree.

_____ Master's degree.

_____ Doctoral degree.

Identify:

1. Specific degree or specialization
   required: _____
   _____
   _____

2. Specific professional license, certificate, or registration required: _____
   _____
   _____

Exhibit 10-1 continued

B. Experience and Training: Note amount of relevant experience necessary to *start* this job.

Previous work experience required:

_____ Zero to three months.

_____ Three to six months.

_____ Six months to one year.

_____ One to three years.

_____ Three to five years of progressively more responsible experience required.

_____ More than five years of progressively responsible work experience required.

Specific kinds of skills required (for example, typing 80 wpm, word processing, basic shop math). *Do not* indicate skills that are not *absolutely necessary* to perform the job.

_____
_____

Specify alternative combinations of education and experience appropriate for recruitment to this position.

_____
_____

C. Given the above minimum requirements, how long would it take for a new hire to become fully functional in the position?

_____

PART III:

A. Frequency of supervision this position receives (check one):

_____ Specific assignments accompanied by clear, detailed, specific instruction.

_____ Specific instructions for new, difficult, or unusual assignments, including suggested work methods.

_____ Assignments defining objectives, priorities, and deadlines.

_____ Specific assignments only in unusual situations not covered fully by existing procedures.

_____ Supervisor sets objectives, sets deadlines with employee.

_____ Supervisor and employee jointly develop objectives and set deadlines.

_____ Supervisor specifies expected results for independently functioning employee.

Exhibit 10-1 continued

Respond to B and C only if this position will supervise others

B. Check activities included in this position's supervisory duties:

__ Hiring	__ Counseling
__ Orienting	__ Directing
__ Training	__ Evaluating Performance
__ Scheduling	__ Promoting
__ Financial Control	__ Disciplining
__ Terminating	__ Other (specify)

C. Responsibility and Accountability

1. Which best describes this position?

   __ Department Head/Administrator/Chief of Service

   __ Manager

   __ First-Line Supervisor

   __ Working Leader

2. Number of employees *evaluated* by this position._____

3. Number of *supervisory* employees reporting to this position._____

4. Total number of employees for which this position is responsible._____

5. Percent of daily time spent in supervision._____

6. Briefly describe other measures of accountability applicable to this position:_____

Exhibit 10-1 continued

PART IV:

A. Work Environment:
Identify physical effort or mental or visual demands associated with this position such as patient handling, movement of equipment, work requiring continuous attention to details (data entry, transcription, or work performed under constant pressure).

Activity	*Hours Per Day*
_____	_____
_____	_____
_____	_____
_____	_____

B. Working Conditions:
List potentially disagreeable conditions inherent in this job.

Conditions	*Hours Per Day*
Noise	_____
Odor	_____
Adverse Weather	_____
Other (identify)	_____

_____

_____

_____

C. On the average, how many overtime hours per pay period are expected of someone in this position?

_____

D. Estimate the average number of on-call shifts to be expected per month. _____

E. Note other information, not requested in the foregoing pages, that you believe will be helpful in fully describing and evaluating this position. _____

_____

_____

Exhibit 10-1 continued

PART V:

ORGANIZATION CHART

Title of position
to which this
position reports.

Reviewed position.

Written by_____

Approved by _____   Date_____

- *Proposed position title.* If the analysis concerns a proposed new position, the manager completing the analysis should provide a suggested title for the position.

Part I: Position Objectives, Activities and Responsibilities

A. *Position objectives: Briefly state the principal purpose or the primary objectives of the position.* This should simply call for a summary, preferably in a single sentence, of why the position in question should exist in the organization. For example, the objectives of the position of employee benefits manager might be: to develop, implement, and administer employee benefits programs and to recommend policies governing the provision and administration of various employee benefit programs.

B. *Briefly list, in order of importance, the activities performed by the incumbent of this position. Begin each activity statement with a specific active verb that best describes the activity under consideration.* Ideally, the list of activities comprising the position should not exceed nine or ten items. Associated with each activity should be the manager's best indication of how often that activity is performed (such as hourly, four times daily, daily, twice a week, etc.). The significant data elements being gathered are activities and activity frequency. There are few positions that cannot be described adequately in terms of ten or fewer activities. It is possible to list far more than ten activities associated with even a relatively simple position by attempting to capture everything that is likely to be done in the normal course of work. However, one should resist the temptation to describe a job in such detail that the resulting description includes two or three dozen activities. Rather, infrequently encountered activities (such as, for example, a brief task that takes only 30 minutes every three months but is nevertheless necessary) should be combined with other infrequently encountered activities in one or two summary activity statements.

It is important to note the necessity for action statements in describing work activities. It has been all too easy in the past for documents originally purported to be job descriptions to emerge as more philosophical or conceptual statements than actual descriptions. It is absolutely necessary that each activity be described as something people do. To this end it is helpful to supply the user of the position analysis instrument with an array of suggested active verbs.

C. *Describe the direct interpersonal contacts required of a person in this position both inside the organization and outside of the organization.* For a majority of health care organization employees, inside contacts ordinarily would include regular contacts with other departments and their personnel, and with patients, physicians, and visitors. Outside contacts would ordinarily include vendors' representatives, government and social agencies, and perhaps consultants, contractors, attorneys, insurance companies, and such.

D. *Describe the degree, impact, and correctability of errors that can occur in the performance of this job.* This area of information is solicited primarily to give those involved in the job evaluation process the wherewithal to begin to assess responsibility and accountability. However, it also figures actively in the performance appraisal process because it has a direct bearing on the standards an employee will be required to perform against. For example, regarding some particular noncritical task an employee may be given a certain amount of acceptable leeway for error, while in regard to a critical activity there may be no allowable room for error.

Part II: Preparation, Training, and Experience

A. *What would be the minimum level of knowledge required of an individual to qualify for this position (check one).*
   __ Basic knowledge of arithmetic, English, and grammar; the ability to follow simple instructions for which interpretation is not required.
   __ High school diploma or equivalent.
   __ High school diploma or equivalent plus an additional year of special training (or an equivalent of one to three years of practical trade training).
   __ Two year college degree or equivalent, or completion of an accredited apprenticeship program.
   __ Four year college degree.
   __ Master's degree.
   __ Doctoral degree.

In addition, identify:
   1. *Specific degree or specialization required.* The manager should indicate in this section the specific degree or academic major required. For example, a particular nursing position may require a nurse with a four year degree (BSN), so *four year college degree* would be checked above and *nursing* would be indicated under specific degree or specialization; a particular position in biomedical engineering may require a two year degree (AAS) with a major in electronics technology, so *two year college degree or equivalent* would be checked and *electronics*—or perhaps even *biomedical technology*—may be identified under specific degree or specialization.
   2. *Specific professional license, certificate, or registration required.* In response to this item the manager completing the position analysis

should enter the appropriate credentials required by the position, indicating, for example, a nursing license (RN) for a nursing position, or registration as a registered record administrator (RRA) for a particular medical record position.

B. *Indicate the amount of relevant experience necessary for an applicant to have to start in this position.*

Previous work experience:

__ Zero to three months.

__ Three to six months.

__ Six months to one year.

__ One to three years.

__ Three to five years of progressively more responsible work experience.

__ More than five years of progressively more responsible work experience.

1. *Indicate the specific kinds of skills required.* If the individual who is to fill the job in question is going to have to do a considerable amount of typing, for example, in response to this data item the manager might enter: "Type 80 words per minute." Other specific skills such as computer keyboarding ability, offset press operation, or switchboard operation, to name but a few, should be called for here as appropriate. However, the manager completing the analysis should take care to avoid calling for skills that are not absolutely necessary in the basic performance of the job at the level of the normal probationary employee. That is, the manager should take care to distinguish between job skills that are absolutely necessary and other skills that may perhaps be nice to have on this particular job.

2. *Specify alternative combinations of education and experience that may be appropriate to consider for recruiting in this position.* This section is intended to assist the applicant search process by allowing those who do recruiting and screening some flexibility in dealing with otherwise viable candidates who seem not to fit into the slots as outlined above. For example, a particular position ordinarily may be recruited for by asking for someone with a bachelor of science degree and at least one year's experience, and that ordinarily may have proven to be successful in recruiting, but the manager has also recognized that an applicant who has several years—say eight or ten years—of highly appropriate experience would not be excluded from consideration simply because he or she had only a two year degree. This gives the manager, and thus the organization's recruiters, the opportunity to factor some common sense trade offs into their consideration of a job candidate.

C. *Given the foregoing minimum requirements, how long would it take a new employee to become fully functional in this position?* Granted this may be only the crudest of estimates, amounting to no more than an educated guess, but it nevertheless provides some idea of the learning curve involved in getting up to speed in this particular position. In making this estimate, the manager needs to consider that he or she would be starting with a person who is at least minimally qualified in terms of the requirements already specified. Also, caution on the part of the manager completing the analysis is advised in estimating this period. The length of time specified should relate to how long it would take a person to learn to perform consistently at an acceptable level, and should in no way reflect an expectation of the time it would take the person to attain expert status.

Part III: Supervision

A. *Check the most applicable of the following to describe the amount of supervision required by an employee working in this position*:
   __ Specific assignments are accompanied by clear, detailed, specific instructions.
   __ Specific instructions are provided ordinarily only for new, difficult, or unusual assignments, and include suggested work methods.
   __ Assignments are provided that define objectives, establish priorities, and set deadlines.
   __ Specific assignments are provided in only unusual situations that are not covered fully by existing procedures.
   __ The supervisor establishes objectives, and the supervisor and employee jointly determine deadlines.
   __ The supervisor and employee jointly develop objectives and establish deadlines.
   __ The supervisor specifies only the results expected of an independently functioning employee.

   The foregoing seven choices—and there are certainly ways of accomplishing the same ends in a different number of items, perhaps differently expressed—run the complete range from close supervision of an employee whose activities are largely guided and very tightly controlled, to the functioning of a nearly completely autonomous employee. This information can prove helpful in the recruiting process, has implications for performance appraisal as well, and is absolutely essential in the job evaluation process.

B. *Managerial Duties: Indicate those of the following activities that would constitute part of this position's supervisory or managerial duties.* This is intended to provide a simple reading of the degree to which the employee filling this position will be expected to perform supervisory or managerial duties. Although it will at first seem obvious that a great many, if not the majority, of managerial positions will involve essentially all of the following, some supervisory positions (such as a team leader or working group leader) will involve less than the complete list. For example, a working group leader may be involved in orienting, directing, counseling, and some of the others, but may have no role in certain activities such as scheduling, budgeting and control, or disciplining.

_____ Hiring	_____ Counseling
_____ Orienting	_____ Directing
_____ Training	_____ Evaluating Performance
_____ Scheduling	_____ Promoting
_____ Budgeting and Control	_____ Disciplining
_____ Terminating	_____ Other (Identify)

C. *Responsibility and accountability:*

   1. Which of the following best describes this position?

   __ Department head or administrator or chief of service.

   __ Manager.

   __ First-line supervisor.

   __ Working group leader.

   __ Other.

   2. Indicate the number of employees who are evaluated by the person in this position. _____

   3. Indicate the number of supervisory employees reporting to the person in this position. _____

   4. Indicate the total number of employees for whom the person in this position is ultimately responsible._____

   5. Indicate the percentage of daily time it is necessary for the person in this position to spend in supervisory activity. _____

   6. Briefly describe other measures of accountability applicable in describing this position. Appropriate to mention as other measures of accountability include necessary references to the clear and direct responsibility for life, safety, cash, or property. For example, the approximate amount of the individual's potential budget responsibility could be indicated here, as can an individual's responsibility for the protection of confidential information.

There is a certain amount of intentional overlap between and among the foregoing half-dozen data items. Not all management terms and labels mean the same to all people; for example, one individual's notions of supervisor and manager could be exactly the reverse of another person's ideas. Also, people are frequently led in one direction or another by the use of terms such as supervisor, manager, or department head as both generic labels and actual organizational titles.

In asking different but overlapping questions about numbers of employees viewed in various contexts, it is possible, when this information is combined with organization chart detail, to cut through variations in differing perceptions and arrive at factual information. A surprisingly high number of middle managers for example, are inclined to confuse the number of people directly reporting to them with the total number of people for whom they are responsible. The overlapping nature of these data requests allows evaluators to sort out the numbers for what they truly represent.

The manager completing a position analysis for a first-line or charge-type supervisory employee might find that no fixed number of employees can be indicated as reporting to this position. For example, an employee who works as a staff person three days a week and then serves as charge on weekends over four or five people will have varying supervisory responsibilities. For such a position, the total number of employees for whom the person in this position is responsible may have to be indicated as "zero to five."

Part IV: Environment, Conditions, and Other Factors

This section calls for gathering much of the information that would go into the working conditions part of a job evaluation. However, also included are a number of points of information that some job applicants would like to know in considering whether to accept employment, and that the hiring manager would like the applicant to know so as to provide assurance that the person is being given full information on which to make a decision.

A. *Work environment: Identify physical effort or mental or visual demands associated with this position, such as patient handling, movement of equipment, work requiring continuous concentration on detail, or work that is performed under constant pressure.* Here it would be helpful to enter job factors such as: frequency of patient handling (constant lifting, occasional lifting, etc.), two to four hours each day at a video display terminal, eight hours a day at a high-activity switchboard, six to eight hours a day of material distribution throughout the facility, occasional lifting of forty pounds or more, and the like.

B. *Working conditions: Indicate all potentially disagreeable conditions inherent in the performance of this position.* Here the manager completing the analysis should list factors such as: exposure to noise from (what) for (however many hours a day), exposure to noxious odors (with estimated duration or frequency), estimated exposure to adverse weather conditions (pertinent to all employees who must move in and out of the building in the course of work), and other potentially disagreeable or possibly dangerous factors such as heat, radiation, or infection.

C. *On the average, how many overtime hours per two week pay period are expected of an employee in this position?*
D. *On the average, how many on-call shifts per month are likely to be required of an employee in this position?*
E. *List or otherwise describe any other items of importance that you believe have not been accounted for appropriately in the foregoing sections, and which you believe should receive consideration in recruiting for and evaluating this position.*

Part V: Organization Chart

Provide a simple organization chart showing the organizational relationships of the position being analyzed. The position appearing at the top of the organization chart should be the position to which an employee working in the position being analyzed will directly report. If the position being analyzed is nonsupervisory, the organization chart will depict only two levels. However, other positions that also report directly to the same managerial position should also be depicted. If the position being analyzed is that of a supervisor or manager, in addition to depicting the upward reporting relationship it is necessary for the chart to show the complete network of reporting relationships leading up to the position being analyzed.

An organization chart remains the simplest available means of depicting reporting relationships in the work situation. Also, when considered in conjunction with the information obtained in answer to the questions in Part III, the organization chart will frequently enable one to resolve questions that might have arisen in the effort to interpret the data entered in Part III.

PROCESS: DEVELOPMENT AND APPLICATION

As mentioned earlier, a working group assembled to develop the organization's position analysis should consist of certain human resource professionals and a number of managers. Further, the group should be chaired by one of the managers but should have staff support (draft typing and distribution, meeting scheduling, and such) provided by the human resource department. Once the group is formally assembled and the task made clear to the members, the development process can proceed approximately as follows:

• Pooling the knowledge and preferences available in the group, a working outline would be created. This might consist, for example, of general descriptions of the six separate parts of the position analysis presented on the preceding pages.

- Following general agreement on an outline, a first draft would be developed. This might be addressed adequately by the group as a whole, but it could prove easier to compartmentalize the task by assigning first draft responsibility for a couple of outline sections to each of several subgroups of two or three people each.
- Once a complete first draft is assembled, all group members should be called on to critique the entire draft. This critique should be accomplished by each group member working independently and ideally should be done between regular meetings of the group.
- Merging the individual critiques at a group meeting, the group should attempt to develop a second draft that is acceptable to all members. This draft should be critiqued individually as was the first, and again any differences should be resolved by the entire group. This draft process should continue, as necessary, through further iterations until an acceptable final draft is in hand.
- At this stage it would be helpful to secure the assistance of several other supervisors and managers (perhaps five or six) who are not involved in the development process, and have each of them complete a sample position analysis. It is best if such sample analyses are undertaken on well-known, well-populated positions (such as staff nurse, housekeeping worker, or food service worker) that are not currently known to require significant change. These sample analyses would then be reviewed by the working group to assure that all of the various information needs the position analysis is intended to fill are indeed met.
- One additional step might be in order. Consider circulating the agreed-on final version to all members of the organization's management group, much in the manner that a new policy and procedure might be circulated for comment prior to publication. The development group need not feel bound to include every change or addition that might result from such review (certainly a review of any document by perhaps several dozen persons of varying needs and perspectives can bring in so many differences of opinion that complete reconciliation is impossible) but the group may nevertheless discover that some previously unnoticed legitimate needs have emerged.
- Once finalized, the position analysis should be furnished to all managerial personnel along with complete instructions for its use.

A great deal of information is called for in a position analysis, and completing one can sometimes require much thought and effort. However, once a thorough position analysis is available for a given job:

- efficient job evaluation can take place, and the job can be placed in an appropriate grade in the compensation structure

- simple but totally adequate employment specifications can be extracted readily
- simple, straightforward, task-related job descriptions can be developed, job descriptions that can apply directly in criteria-based performance appraisal without the need for one to fish out and clarify the criteria
- specific orientation and training needs can be identified readily

A finished position analysis is often a sizeable document, occasionally running as long as six or seven pages. However, without a separate position analysis there has been a tendency for job descriptions to become longer and more detailed, themselves often becoming documents of four, five, or more pages. Many organizations' systems require that job descriptions be reviewed and updated annually, so some organizations have found themselves frequently reissuing multipage job descriptions. But a six- or seven-page position analysis rarely if ever needs to be reissued. Since it is a source document only it rarely leaves the files, and changes that occur can be noted informally on the original. A position analysis should be redone only if some dramatic change occurs, perhaps change of a magnitude that clearly indicates a change in pay grade or a change in level of reporting responsibilities (such as a nonsupervisory position that is converted into a supervisory position).

In most instances a six- or seven-page position analysis will give rise to one or more single-page job descriptions. A one-page job description can be updated regularly as necessary with task-specific information without having to alter or reissue the position analysis. In this manner the organization is able to gather and retain all pertinent information about any given position while still being able to maintain concise task-specific job descriptions that are completely up to date at all times. And it is concise task-specific job descriptions, completely up to date at all times, that feed and support the critical process of criteria-based performance appraisal.

11

Job Descriptions and Job Specifications*

A TOOL FOR TOO MANY USES

The job description is well known, and in many instances well accepted, as a primary management vehicle for communicating the duties, responsibilities, scope of authority, organizational relationships, and personnel qualifications for each job in the organization. Although it is well known and perhaps well accepted, it is just as likely to be ignored for long periods of time. When suddenly called on, it is found to be either lacking with respect to the needs of the moment or top-heavy with extraneous information.

In most health care organizations, job descriptions have been called on to serve a growing number of different purposes. As the number of uses of the job description has increased, so too has the amount of information conveyed in the job description increased. The variety and detail of the information captured in many of today's job descriptions have expanded such that this increasingly important instrument now often serves many of its purposes in crude and clumsy fashion. The growth of the job description has been the growth of a supposedly universal tool. Too often, today's job description attempts to do so much that it ultimately does little or nothing well. The job description has progressed in the manner of the person who tries so hard to please everyone that eventually no one at all is pleased.

JOB DESCRIPTION USES

The job description has specific applicability in recruitment and placement, employee compensation, employee orientation and training, organizational

*An earlier version of this chapter appeared as Charles R. McConnell, "Job Descriptions: Convenient Generics and Essential Specifics," *The Health Care Supervisor,* vol. 7 no. 1 (October 1988) pp. 76–84.

development, and employee performance appraisal. It is also becoming increasingly important as a factor in some organizations' entanglements with employment legislation and other laws.

Recruitment and Placement

The job description is frequently the starting point for a number of activities related to recruitment and placement. From the job description recruiters or personnel representatives extract information comprising what might be described as an employment specification. This specification identifies the job in terms of the kind of work involved, the qualifications required or desired of candidates, and the general conditions of employment (work hours and such). This information then is reflected to whatever extent may be considered necessary in a job posting or an advertisement.

The job description is also likely to feature prominently in a recruiter's screening interview or a supervisor's placement interview with a job candidate. There are few better ways of bringing a candidate quickly up to speed on the requirements of an open position than to review an up-to-date job description with a knowledgeable interviewer. In brief, the recruitment and placement function of the job description is to ensure that both interviewer and candidate have ready access to detailed knowledge of the job's functions and requirements.

Employee Compensation

Once established, any job in the organization must be subjected to some form of job evaluation. Regardless of whether this job evaluation is a formal process (such as point-factor analysis, in which points are assigned to various characteristics of the job) or an informal process (such as subjective ranking with other jobs), it requires some reasonably thorough record of the major elements of the job. More often than not this record is the job description.

It is the job evaluation, formal or informal, that establishes the job's placement in the compensation system and thus determines its pay range. Since the job description fuels the job evaluation, the job description is directly related to compensation. Indeed, the organization's structure of job descriptions provides a consistent basis for the organization's wage structure.

Employee Orientation and Training

Up-to-date job descriptions are invaluable aids in orienting new employees to the job. Although they are insufficient in and of themselves—the most important part of job orientation remains that which is obtained from people, not from documents—job descriptions nevertheless provide ready reference information about job content that new employees can refer to again and again. An employee who thoroughly studies the position's job description upon first starting work will usually have a running start on learning the job via personal instruction.

The job description is frequently of value in remedial instruction or reorientation in the case of an employee who appears in need of improved understanding of the duties of the job.

The organization's body of job descriptions, when considered in divisions or groups of similarly graded or similarly constituted jobs, is applicable in educational planning. From this body of information it is possible to extract common needs that then may be addressed through continuing education. To cite a simple example, all job descriptions that cite employee needs for working knowledge of cardiopulmonary resuscitation (CPR) allow those responsible for education to plan CPR training based on the extent of total needs.

Organizational Development

Under the heading of organizational development, which includes reshaping elements of the organization as needed, maintaining organizational elements in an appropriate relationship with the health care business environment, and maintaining consistency with the dynamic goals of the organization, we are likely to find a number of functions not readily considered as uses of the job description. Regarding organizational development, the individual and collective parts of a complete, up-to-date job description structure can be used:

- to establish the interrelationships of various jobs in the organization, assuring unity of command (one of the supporting principles of the basic management function of organizing) in the avoidance of functional gaps and overlaps
- as a general aid in reorganizing a work unit or entire organization
- to appropriately apportion authority and responsibility among employees
- to delineate lines of promotion
- to aid in maintaining operating continuity in the face of change
- to delineate the organization's formal channels of communication
- as an activity baseline for operations auditing (the process of assessing how well an organization or work unit is performing relative to requirements or expectations)
- as a starting point for methods improvement study activity
- as a basis for human resources planning (the process of projecting short-term and long-term human resource needs)

Employee Performance Appraisal

In recent years the emphasis of performance appraisal has appropriately shifted from personality-based appraisal to criteria-based appraisal and other forms of evaluation based on job-description requirements. There has been an increasing need to evaluate employees not on what they are but rather on what they do, and what an employee does (or is expected to do) is best captured in a complete, up-to-date job description.

The shift in appraisal emphasis is not accidental, nor is it entirely optional. The Joint Commission on Accreditation of Healthcare Organizations calls specifically for criteria-based performance appraisal in its standards governing nursing service. Also, the regulations of a number of state health departments likewise dictate criteria-based appraisal.

A functionally oriented job description provides the basis for criteria-based performance appraisal. By providing a record of the tasks an employee is expected to perform and the results expected from task performance, the job description makes it possible for an evaluator to better compare what the employee actually does with what should be done.

Accurate job descriptions also facilitate performance appraisal using systems other than today's popular criteria-based approaches. For example, the process of joint target setting, in which an employee and immediate supervisor agree on a set of improvement targets developed largely by the employee, depends on a current job description to define normal expectations of performance (see Chapter 15). Similarly, management by objectives (MBO) depends on the baseline of a current job description. One can frame realistic objectives beyond so-called normal performance only upon first knowing what constitutes normal performance.

Criteria-based or task-based appraisal is here to stay, and personality-based appraisal will continue its journey into the past. Therefore, the job description will continue to take on increasing importance in its need to be a concise, accurate rendering of the tasks an employee is expected to perform and the results the employee is expected to achieve.

Legal Implications

Since the early to middle 1960s the job description has been taking on significance in many employers' encounters with various federal and state laws governing employment practices. Although it began slowly and unnoticeably (except to a few employers who began to find that their job descriptions were being used against them in employment discrimination cases), the job description's legal significance recently has been increasing at an alarming rate.

It is now common for the job description to be entered into legal proceedings concerned with charges of discrimination based on sex, race, age, or other conditions. A job description may or may not be used by a plaintiff's attorney depending on what the attorney wishes to prove. Nevertheless, a job description used in a legal action is frequently assumed to be the official record of the job. If the job description is out of date—if it fails to include tasks that are actually part of the job, or if it includes tasks that are no longer part of the job—it may well be used against the organization by a plaintiff who is attempting to establish discrimination. This application of the job description is especially likely in the pursuit of claims filed under the Equal Pay Act of 1963.

Since many supervisors and managers still regard the job description as an annoyance under most circumstances and often as only a write-it, file-it, forget-it document, they run an increasing risk of being trapped by their department's job descriptions. An accurate, up-to-date job description is often the supervisor's best defense against legal action. Conversely, an outdated job description can be one of a plaintiff's attorney's most useful weapons.

In an institution that is undergoing a union organizing campaign, accurate job descriptions are important in determining whether certain personnel are or are not eligible for inclusion in the proposed bargaining unit. Since eligibility for such inclusion determines eligibility to vote in the representation election, current job descriptions can be critical in management's counter-organizing activities. If the institution already has a union in place, the description of a proposed new position often will be critical in determining whether the position will be union-covered or nonunion.

Also, the job description for a proposed position will frequently be used in determining whether the position will be exempt or nonexempt regarding the overtime provisions of the Fair Labor Standards Act.

TOO MANY USES

One need not ponder the foregoing paragraphs too long to be able to cite even more constructive uses for the job description. That is precisely the major problem with many of today's job descriptions—they have been broadened in scope, content, and detail to such an extent that they address many needs overall but serve most of these needs inefficiently. Few if any of the foregoing uses of the job description require all of the data the job description is likely to provide.

Many of the job description's uses (for example, determining employment specifications and establishing a pay grade) are one-time activities or are performed infrequently at best. However, a few important uses—those that actively involve the individual employee—are regularly recurring and require specifically targeted job information.

Job descriptions in many organizations have become all-purpose generic documents that have grown to satisfy all needs. In places it is not unusual to find job descriptions that run to five, six, or more pages in length. In addition, since even the most comprehensive job description cannot account for all of the likely variations on specific kinds of positions, we are also likely to find large numbers of job descriptions that are quite similar, but not identical, to each other.

Consider, for example, the institution of more than 2,000 employees that maintained approximately 500 job descriptions in its active files. Since each job description utilized a "standard" format 7 pages long, each of the 500 job descriptions was comprised of at least 7 sheets of paper. Among these 500 job descriptions were 15 for the position of medical secretary in various departments (for example, medical secretary—cardiology; medical secretary—gastrointestinal; medical secretary—obstetrics/gynecology; and so on).

The 15 medical secretary positions were all variations on the same position. All were in the same pay grade. The briefest task list on any of the job descriptions consisted of 9 items; the longest consisted of 12 items. Of the tasks listed on the 15 descriptions, *8 items were common to all 15 positions*. In addition, with very few exceptions the qualifications and working conditions for all 15 positions were identical. Considering the total contents of these 15 seven-page job descriptions, the 15 positions were approximately 95 percent identical.

Why 15 separate job descriptions instead of a single document? This condition developed for an essentially sound reason. When the institution adopted criteria-based performance appraisal it was necessary to provide an accurate job description rendering each separate medical secretary's exact duties. How else would one be able thoroughly to appraise a secretary on job-description tasks unless those tasks all appeared on the job description?

It has thus been the adoption of criteria-based appraisal that has channelled the job description into becoming thoroughly task specific. And it has been the adherence to the continued use of the job description in all of its other legitimate applications that has turned it into a lengthy, sometimes cumbersome document. The job description's many traditional uses caused it to become a broad, generic vehicle; its newer use in criteria-based appraisal has necessitated its becoming specific as well.

Although we always should think twice about adding to the varieties of paperwork with which we must work, we nevertheless might conclude that another layer of documentation could be justified in better serving all of the necessary purposes of today's job description.

THE POSITION ANALYSIS, JOB FAMILIES, AND THE "NEW" JOB DESCRIPTION

In the preceding chapter an instrument referred to as the *position analysis* was introduced. The position analysis is intended to include all information about a given position that could conceivably be needed for any purpose in the organization. In short, the position analysis would serve as the primary source document—indeed, in most cases the sole source document—for satisfying all of the job description uses cited in the earlier sections of this presentation. And the position analysis becomes a fully complete source document if we add but one more use to those already cited—the creation of a job description or job specification (see Figure 11–1).

The basic need being addressed through the recommended creation of an added layer of documentation is twofold: the need to facilitate all of the foregoing uses of job information and the need to provide concise, specific job information to support criteria-based performance appraisal.

Adding a Document to Reduce Total Paper

Recommending the addition of yet another document to the papermill of operations may seem like modern management heresy. Surely the more conscientious would feel that we should be eliminating forms, not proliferating them. However, the present instance is one in which the addition of one layer of documentation, along with a simple change in concept, can lead to a streamlined system that operates on considerably less total paper.

The simple concept referred to is that of job families. Within most health care organizations there are a number of possible groupings of similar jobs. A grouping of essentially similar jobs comprises a job family. All that is required to define a job family is a number of positions that are similar in the kind of work performed or the basic skill employed and that are identical in pay grade.

To resurrect an earlier example, the 15 medical secretary positions comprise a job family. These positions all reside in the same pay grade and all require application of essentially the same skills. Therefore, instead of 15 seven-page "job descriptions" to be created, filed, updated, copied, distributed, and applied to various uses, there need be just *one* six- or seven-page position analysis for the *job family* of medical secretary that in turn spawns 15 one-page job descriptions or job specifications, one for each medical secretarial position (medical secretary—cardiology, etc.). (The term "job specification" is deliberately introduced as interchangeable with "job description." The management of an organization adopting this approach might prefer to adopt job specification and altogether eliminate reference to the job description because of some deeply

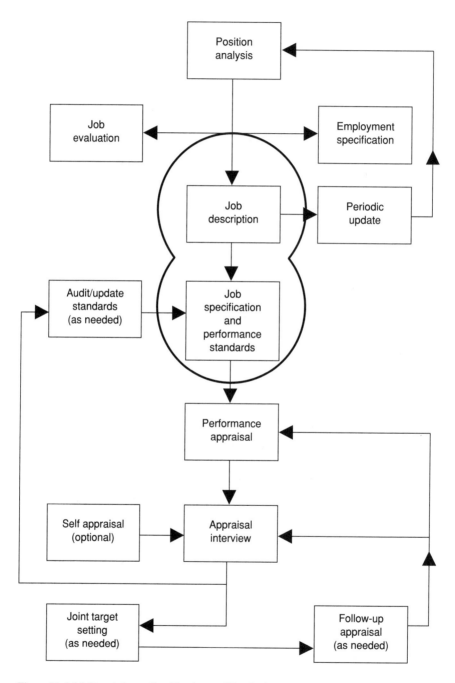

Figure 11–1 Job Description to Specifications and Standards

entrenched—and, under this approach, incorrect—notions of the nature of a job description.)

Following the same reasoning applied to the position of medical secretary, in that same organization a number of other combinations are possible. For example: in the building services department at least five jobs could be grouped into one job family (building service worker); five or six laboratory positions could be gathered into one job family (laboratory technologist); 10 or 12 nursing positions could be collected into a job family for Staff Nurse; and three somewhat differentiated but similarly graded positions in human resources could be gathered in a job family for personnel representative.

There would be a number of job families for which a position analysis led to only one job specification. For example, the finance division will have only one position titled controller, so the controller position analysis would be for a family of one and lead to a single job specification; the institution might have three painters in the maintenance department, all of whom perform identical duties, so the position analysis for painter would also lead to a single job specification.

Adopting the job family concept and the job specification, the previously mentioned institution having some 500 lengthy job descriptions could cover its 2,000-plus member work force with approximately 150 position analyses and 500 one-page job specifications. In doing so, the total amount of paper involved would be reduced dramatically and the amount of filing, copying, and transmitting would accurately encapsulate the duties of each position in a manner fully supportive of the needs of criteria-based performance appraisal.

JOB SPECIFICATION CONTENTS

At the heart of the job specification lies a concise listing of the duties of the individual in the position. These duties should be described briefly, in order of their importance. (Order of importance generally will parallel the order of time consumed; that is, one's most important function usually will also consume the largest amount of that person's time when compared with other functions.) All statements of duties should be action statements that clearly indicate what the person should do or the results the person should produce. The action nature of these statements of duties must be stressed; the job specification has no room for the philosophical niceties found in many older job descriptions or that even, on occasion, might be allowed to creep into the position analysis.

For example, the first two duties on the job specification for Laundry Aide might appear as:

1. Collect linen and garments from assigned areas; sort, weigh, and record weights. (Daily for areas assigned per schedule.)

2. Sort contents of each hamper and segregate and bundle items requiring special stain removal treatment. (Daily for soiled laundry hampers transported to laundry.)

The duties listed on the job specification should encompass all of what the employee is expected to do during a normal work week (or perhaps two or four weeks, if a specific, regularly recurring number of duties is known). However, it is not necessary to capture all infrequently done tasks in the job specification. As long as the basic list of duties encompasses 90 to 95 percent of the employee's work there will be a sufficient basis for performance appraisal. It is certainly not necessary to have a specific line dedicated to a known task that requires, for example, about 15 minutes once every six months. Regarding known but infrequent tasks, and tasks that are completely unknown until they arise, it is sufficient to employ statements like the following:

- other scheduled tasks: quarterly turnover report; semiannual employee meeting; departmental staff meeting
- special assignments or other related tasks as assigned by supervision

Other information on the job specification may vary from organization to organization but would logically include: job title, department, job grade, and date of the job specification. Regarding date, it is perhaps wise to carry both the date of original issue and the date of the most recent revision. However, if only one date is used it should be the date of the most recent revision. Copies of documents like the job description or job specification tend to languish in files and desks after they have become outdated. Consider the number of times you may have picked up a copy of a job description and wondered whether it is current.

The job specification should also include some direct reference, usually by title and number, to the position analysis for the job family on which it is based.

While there can be a short section of the job specification devoted to special concerns as necessary, there is no need to include all other so-called standard job description information (such as, for example, education, experience requirements, working conditions, and the like) that appear on the position analysis. Again, the heart of the job specification is a concise listing of job duties sufficient to serve two important purposes: to provide the employee with specific knowledge of what is expected in the way of job performance and to provide the supervisor and employee with the means to participate in criteria-based performance appraisal.

"FINISHED" IS ONLY STARTED

A fully implemented job specification forms the basis for criteria-based performance appraisal by providing a concise, performance-oriented task listing for each employee. This will assure that appraisal proceeds completely in consideration of job-related criteria.

However, truly effective, legally defensible performance appraisal must relate what is to be done with how much is done or how well it is done. The job specification satisfies the what of performance appraisal by establishing task-based criteria to the exclusion of personality considerations. However, the job specification does not address how much or how well; it still falls to the supervisor to assess judgmentally the employee's performance relative to each criterion (on scales such as unsatisfactory, satisfactory, above satisfactory, outstanding, etc.).

What is needed in conjunction with the job specification to fully implement effective and legally defensible performance appraisal is a set of performance standards for each job specification. Criteria-based appraisal can be implemented using job specifications and supervisors' judgmental assessments of performance. Following such implementation, performance standards then can be developed on an ongoing basis over a period of several years, moving the organization toward a point at which each employee eventually can be evaluated to a significant extent using objective standards.

It should be possible to reach a stage of system maturity at which the majority of nonprofessional employees have performance standards for 75 percent or more of their duties and professional and managerial employees have performance standards for as much as 50 percent of their duties. The continuing development of performance standards becomes a legitimate part of appraisal system maintenance.

12

Objective Measurement in Appraisal*

ENTER "STANDARDS OF PERFORMANCE"

Appraisal yesterday as compared with appraisal today, and even present appraisal in one organization as compared with appraisal in another, suggests a continuous scale of appraisal approaches. This scale begins with totally subjective appraisal, evaluation based on opinions, beliefs, impressions, and feelings. At the other end of the scale lies objective appraisal, that is, evaluation based largely on measurements, data, and facts. In improving the quality, reliability, fairness, and legal defensibility of performance appraisal, we should aspire to be moving continually away from feeling and toward fact in improving appraisal processes.

It is in the third phase of the evolution of performance appraisal (as described in Chapter 1) that measurement and measurability become extremely important. The criteria against which employees are to be assessed must, whenever possible, be reasonably measurable; and reasonable means of measurement should be provided for most performance criteria.

Given the practical manner in which appraisal has been developing, the age-old vertical scale—the list of requirements against which a person is evaluated—is becoming composed of just two kinds of elements:

1. specific task steps for which output can be measured in absolute terms
2. discretely identified criteria that permit assessment of narrow areas of performance in simple terms (for example, something that can be said to have been done or not done, or reference to a so-called standard that can be said to have been not met, met, or exceeded).

In setting out scoring for appraisals, or selecting the elements of the horizontal scale, it is becoming necessary to move away from the traditional multiple judgments of relative success (satisfactory, outstanding, etc.) and replace these with the absolute measures or assessment guidelines referred to above.

---

*Portions of this chapter first appeared in Charles R. McConnell, "In Search of Objective Measurement in Performance Appraisal," *The Health Care Supervisor,* vol. 10, no. 2 (December, 1991) pp. 69–77.

Many of today's concerns with performance appraisal—and many of today's problems and misunderstandings involving appraisal—turn on various interpretations of the meaning of the phrase *standards of performance*. Few job descriptions, even the most thoroughly constructed ones, provide complete, workable standards. Further, there are many difficulties experienced because users of performance appraisal work according to differing interpretations of key appraisal elements, particularly criteria and standards.

A job description element, even one that is appropriately refined for appraisal purposes, is usually a statement of what the employee is expected to do. To serve as a true standard of performance this expression must also include the primary elements of an effective objective, that is:

- what must be done;
- how much must be done;
- when it must be done.

The *when* dimension of a true standard need not always be spelled out specifically, yet it is, if only by implication, a necessary part of the standard. There will be conditions of timeliness or frequency (daily, weekly, etc.) associated with many job description statements, but some of the job's time requirements are legitimately implied as relating to performance of a task as needed, as appropriate, or when directed.

The *what* of a task is ordinarily embodied in the basic job description statement. If the statement includes nothing else, at least it identifies what must be done.

Wanted: Precise Measures

Major weaknesses lie in most of today's appraisal approaches in their inability to provide the evaluator with thoroughly workable guidelines for assessing how much must be done. So-called standards are frequently unclear and often are not seen the same way by employee and evaluator. There is also evidence to suggest that most evaluators cannot accurately distinguish among a variety of performance levels, further suggesting reasons for many managers' discomfort at having to rate employee performance along a six- or seven-choice scale ranging from poor to excellent. It is entirely possible that the majority of evaluators can distinguish comfortably and clearly among just three subjectively assessed levels of performance (for example, poor, satisfactory, and outstanding).[1]

The literature of performance appraisal contains considerable conflict on the use of just three levels of performance. We are told that "behaviorists believe that it is difficult, if not impossible, to consistently identify the correct performance level when more than three categories are being used;" [2] and "...use only three rating distinctions: zero if targets are not met; one when targets are met; and two in cases in which targets are exceeded."[3] However, we are also admonished to "never use a three-point scale, which may place the employee visually in the middle."[4]

There is perhaps some justification in a caution against a central tendency when an evaluator is forced to pick from among just three levels of performance; however, this tendency is likely to be equally prevalent when, for example, five choices are provided.

Even if most of our horizontal rating scales were compressed to three judgments, however, appraisal would continue to generate considerable discomfort for employee and evaluator alike. Although some 80 percent of employees overall can be said to fall into the satisfactory category, the majority of employees believe themselves to be in the top 30 percent of employees or at least above average.[5]

We may desire precise measures for the appraisal process, but we are not going to obtain them in all instances. It is not sufficient to rework the vertical scale in specific detail and refer to a "new criteria-based performance appraisal system." Criteria basing is an admirable and necessary direction, but this must be done recognizing that criteria quite literally are rules, standards, or means of judging. Criteria basing must go beyond the clear delineation of *what* and provide a measure of *how much*. The measure of how much, at its extremes, can be wholly objective or highly subjective; it can be a precise number, a range of value, or a guide for judgment.

DETERMINING WHAT TO MEASURE

The development of effective performance appraisal criteria for a specific position must be preceded by the development of an effective job description (see Chapter 11). The creation of standards of performance must spring from a reasonable job description that lists the majority of activities involved in the particular job.

An effective job description need not be lengthy or overly detailed. It may, rather, consist of 5 or 6 or perhaps no more than 10 or 12 statements that in total encompass most of what the employee is expected to do. It usually need not, and in many instances cannot, include everything that the employee might be called on to do at any time (unless, of course, there exists a contractual requirement to spell out all tasks no matter how insignificant or how infrequently encountered). Listed in either order of importance or order of time consumed (which may or may not be the same), these few descriptions of responsibilities should cover up to 90 or 95 percent of the employee's activity under normal circumstances.

One statement on the job description then might lead to one or several evaluation standards. Keeping in mind for the moment that true criteria or standards include indications of both *what* and *how much*, consider the development of *what* will be evaluated springing from a single point in the job description of an employee working as a courier in a hospital's communications center. The first job description entry is simply:

1. drive hospital vehicles and deliver mail and packages to various locations as required by the posted daily schedule

This single job description entry leads, in this case, to three criteria on which the performance of the task will be judged:

a. complete scheduled morning and afternoon runs within 90 minutes of signing out (as measured by monthly review of courier log)
b. accomplish nonscheduled pickups and deliveries as requested (as assessed by manager)
c. report vehicle problems, traffic difficulties, or unavoidable delays to manager upon returning to hospital (as assessed by manager)

As another example, consider the third job description entry for the position of nursing assistant:

3. provide all patient care in a professional manner

Then examine the four criteria the nursing department established for assessing this one rather broadly stated job description task:

a. maintain a professional appearance at all times
b. observe the hospital's dress code
c. establish and maintain a professional demeanor by demonstrating tact and understanding when dealing with patients, team members, other health practitioners, and the public
d. remain reliable and accountable for all care rendered

In attempting to address something as arguable as "professional manner," these four criteria provide a simplistic breakdown to which one can then apply a simple three-possible-outcome judgment (described in the following section).

When each job description entry is broken down to reasonably simplistic criteria in the foregoing manner, an employee's performance then can be evaluated using a combination of a number of simple objective measures and simple limited-outcome judgments. However, creating these simplistic criteria for all of the job description tasks in the typical health care organization requires considerable writing skill, knowledge of behavioral objectives, and untold amounts of time.

Because of the time, and thus the personnel expense involved in developing evaluation criteria and establishing their measurements, some organizations choose to utilize packaged systems available from consultants, publishers, and other suppliers. Although these systems, which ordinarily include job descriptions as well as evaluation criteria, rarely if ever fit a given organization's exact needs, it is sometimes possible to save considerable time and money by purchasing a packaged system and modifying it to meet the organization's unique needs.

DETERMINING "HOW MUCH" OF "WHAT"

It should be evident from the foregoing examples that total objectivity in measuring performance must remain a theoretical ideal. Regarding the applicability of objective measurement to tasks listed on job descriptions:

- Some tasks can be measured readily in absolute terms.
- Some tasks can never be measured in absolute terms.
- Some tasks can be measured in absolute terms only if costly steps of questionable value are taken to create the measurements.

Ready Made Measurements

For criterion a of the courier evaluation, concerning completion of scheduled runs in the allotted time, for example, the results are measurable with little difficulty. Direct reference to the courier log for a given month ordinarily will reveal whether all runs were completed in the allotted time. Further, if there were variations or questionable circumstances, times when on-time completion was not possible should be identifiable in unusual circumstances reported per criterion c.

For the courier's criterion a it remains only for those designing the evaluation to decide the extent of flexibility that may be allowed. Perhaps the actual expectation becomes: complete all scheduled runs within the allotted time 95 percent to 99 percent of the time. This allows some reasonable slack based on the relative importance of the function. It might be considered, for example, that being 5 percent off is within the normal range of expectation for a courier and that this behavior would cause no real problem, while an error rate of even one-half of one percent might be considered intolerably high for a certain laboratory procedure.

The standards of performance should, as noted above, reflect the relative importance of the task. Depending on its nature a critical element should be accompanied by a requirement for exacting performance leaving little if any room for error. An element can be considered critical when failure to meet it:

- would be life threatening
- would keep other workers from accomplishing their jobs
- would cause or result in significant property damage or loss
- would cause or result in the department or organization not meeting key objectives[6]

As to expressing the measurement so the evaluator can apply it simply, this can be done as easily as supplying the numbers 1, 2, and 3. Again looking at the example of the courier, assessing the employee in regard to criterion 1a (on-time completion rate) can be as simple as circling the appropriate number:

1. on-time completion rate below 95 percent (failed to meet standard)
2. on-time completion rate 95 percent to 99 percent (met standard)
3. on-time completion rate consistently 100 percent (exceeded standard)

This matter of schedule compliance is but a single example of the objective measurement of a task. One can readily identify a number of tasks that lend themselves to measurement with little difficulty.

Measurement at a Cost

It has also been stated that some tasks can be measured in absolute terms only if costly steps of questionable value are taken to create the measurements. It is one consideration to correctly know the nature of a particular measurement; it is another consideration entirely to generate that measurement in a form that is both usable and verifiable.

A performance measure is essentially a work standard (or time standard or productivity indicator, as such might also be called). The creation of a fair, accurate, defensible work standard requires time and effort—usually the application of the skills of industrial engineering or management engineering—and thus money. Is the organization's management going to spend a few weeks or months of engineering resources to create work standards that apply to several hundred staff nurses? Quite likely they may; the expense may seem reasonable in light of the reliable measurements to be gained. However, will the same organization willingly spend even a few days of resources to quantify the evaluation criteria for a single physical therapist or another one-of-a-kind specialized employee? Probably not, so some appraisals will continue to include fewer objective measures than otherwise might be possible.

An institution that already has a work measurement or productivity monitoring system in place has a head start on developing objective measures of individual performance. The outputs of such systems frequently can be adapted to accommodate the needs of performance appraisal comfortably.

In a department that has productivity standards, it generally requires only a modest amount of management engineering assistance to break down the departmental standards into expressions that apply to individual workers. Even if engineered productivity standards and management engineering or other work measurement has not been provided, it is nevertheless possible to establish reasonable rule-of-thumb standards by monitoring output over time and deciding on the level of output that appears to constitute reasonable performance.

It has been suggested already that a standard should not be rigid but ordinarily should represent an acceptable range of performance. Consider the following example: It is determined, either through work measurement or experience and common sense judgment, that a maintenance technician, when assigned to electric motor preventive maintenance, is expected on the average to perform the required maintenance on 12 motors per shift. The standard then might be expressed as 11 to 13 motors per shift. Extending this example to consideration of performance appraisal's horizontal scale, only three ratings are necessary: failed to meet standard, met standard, and exceeded standard. Thus only these three headings are necessary in a great many cases. This particular duty of the maintenance technician may be expressed on the job specification as: "Service electric motors according to preventive maintenance (PM) schedule. Standard— 11 to 13 motors per shift." An entry in the appropriate column would indicate that the employee usually fails to meet the standard, usually meets the standard, or usually exceeds the standard.

Some standards may be utilized even more simply by applying only two ratings that indicate the person did or did not meet the standard. In the case of the file clerk who is expected to remain caught up within one day's worth of filing, the rating need indicate only that the clerk usually did or did not attain this expected level of performance.

It is always possible to construct additional gradations in performance that quantitatively indicate varying degrees of being under or over standard. However, there are hazards in this, as it necessitates far more counting and monitoring by the supervisor. One can draw the performance indicators so finely that it is virtually impossible to measure performance without constantly counting and regularly monitoring a cumbersome number of indicators. If it is not possible to measure performance against standards without excessive effort on the part of the supervisor, or without falling back on pure judgment because measurement is impractical, then the entire process becomes self-defeating and there might as well not be standards.

Although a considerable number of activities can be put "on standard" for a great many employees, in most cases it is not possible, or at least is impractical, to establish objective measures for every duty on an individual's job description. Certainly the organization will have a number of lower-graded positions consisting of a few predictable manual activities, all of which may be measured objectively. However, a great many health care workers, especially technical and professional employees and supervisors, are expected to exercise individual discretion and judgment in their job performance, and their duties are thus not all objectively measurable. Even for some of the more independently functioning health care professionals, however, it is possible, although sometimes only through considerable effort, to establish reasonably objective standards for up to half of their major job duties.

Rarely, then, can an entire job be expressed in criteria that include objective measurements for all functions. Generally, the simpler and more repetitive a job the more likely one can quantify a significant part of its activities. For example, the job of a routine billing clerk who spends each day processing hundreds of the same kind of transactions in the same way can be expressed almost entirely in measurable terms. But a position that is complex and involves varied work (consider most registered nurses and many other allied health professionals) is much less suited to objective measurement, so a much lesser part of such jobs can be described with output standards.

The routine billing clerk might have a target of so many bills per hour. An admitting representative might have a target of a specified number of admissions per shift. A messenger might be measured by a standard of a certain number of completed trips per shift. A worker in central sterile supply might be measured by a standard of so many packs per hour.

Certain other objective measures might consist of primary expressions of quality. For example, typists or word processor operators might find a target error rate among their measurement criteria. Likewise, a laboratory technician might be subject to a target error rate, and a radiology technologist might be expected to work against a target specifying percentage of X-ray retakes.

A standard may also be a simple expression of the completion of a regularly recurring task. For example, a housekeeping worker may be expected to have the main floor corridors cleaned by 9:00 A.M.; a food service aide may be expected to have breakfast trays distributed by 8:00 A.M.; a staff nurse may be expected to have vital signs completed by 8:00 A.M.; and a file clerk may be expected to maintain filing current to within one day at any given time. In every one of these examples the standard is something that is both objective and measurable.

Possible Measures of Performance

As illustrated through the examples used in the foregoing several paragraphs, objective measures of performance ordinarily take the form of expressions that interrelate two or more of four factors: quantity, quality, time, and cost. Using primary expressions of *quantity* some representative work standards might include:

- number of units of service offered per unit of time
- number of items processed per unit of time
- number of tests processed per unit of time
- number of cases handled per unit of time
- percentage (%) of absences
- percentage (%) of employee compliance

Some measures involving primary expressions of quality are:

- percentage (%) of orders completed without error
- percentage (%) of retests necessary
- percentage (%) of avoidable downtime
- error rate (in any process)
- number of citations upon inspection

Some representative work standards using primary expressions of time are:

- number or percentage (%) of targets missed
- number or percentage (%) answered within five days (for example)
- number of days to complete on average
- number of days elapsed after end of month
- total elapsed time
- frequency (as in times per month, per quarter, etc.)

And some measures related primarily to cost are:

- hours to complete task
- cost per unit
- dollars saved per time period
- expenditures per period (as, for example, for overtime)
- percentage (%) variance from budget

The Basic Choice

Job description tasks must be refined to sets of criteria on which the employee will be evaluated, with every criterion simply and specifically delineated so that it is possible to provide either of the following:

- a precise measure of task performance in quantifiable terms
- a simple two-choice (for example, yes or no) or three-choice (for example, standard not met, met, or exceeded) judgment indicating the evaluator's assessment of the employee's level of success.

The latter choice not only recognizes that it may be too costly or too inconvenient to create measures for certain activities, it also recognizes that it is not possible at all to provide measures for a great many activities. Some job requirements can never be measured in absolute terms, yet it remains important to assess how well these requirements are met.

Consider again, for example, the assessment of the "professional manner" in which the nursing assistant's work is performed, specifically statement a, "maintain a professional appearance at all times." Although guidelines for assessing this criterion can be created and disseminated, these are necessarily subjective in nature. We can only hope that a reasonably uniform concept of professional appearance can be communicated to all evaluators so that a consistent assessment of whether someone has not met, met, or exceeded the standard can be made for each employee covered by the nursing assistant job description.

So-called measurement standards, ready made appraisal criteria, and entire performance appraisal systems are available for "off-the-shelf" purchase. However, jobs of similar title and structure are rarely similar enough from one organization to another for generic approaches to apply constructively. Thoroughly applicable criteria cannot be acquired from "stock," but off-the-shelf material can constitute a good start if it then is modified carefully and thoroughly to fit an organization's unique circumstances.

LEGAL IMPLICATIONS

Legal aspects of performance appraisal are thoroughly explored in Chapter 17. At this point it will be sufficient to cite but two or three general precautions.

Many evaluators are discovering that the appraisals they have written and given their employees are increasingly likely to find their way into various court proceedings. Evaluations tend to hold up more under legal scrutiny if all of the information they contain can be justified factually; they tend to crumble under scrutiny if their contents cannot be justified factually.

To be legally defensible a performance appraisal system must be based primarily on objective criteria. There are, fortunately, no actual dictates in law that spell out what an appraisal should or should not contain (at least not yet). However, the more a given appraisal approach is based on objective criteria, the better the position of that approach in the legal arena.

By objective criteria it is generally meant that the basis for evaluation is the job and not the employee. Therefore, leaving the old personality-based vertical scale in the past and ensuring that all assessments can be traced to job description requirements will go a long way toward ensuring legal defensibility.

Much of the rest of an appraisal system's legal defensibility lies in how the system is applied. It is frequently necessary to demonstrate that an appraisal system is applied equally and consistently to all employees covered by that system. For that reason it is extremely important that all evaluators be well trained in the fair and consistent application of the system.

To minimize the potential problems arising from appraisal, the evaluator should:

- always focus on the *results of behavior*, on what the employee *does*—not what the employee *is*—whether using objective measures or subjective criteria
- back up evaluation comments with specifics—examples, results, etc. (Never make a general criticism; rather, cite specific instances to support a conclusion.)
- strive for consistency, keeping in mind such phenomena of evaluation as the tendency for longer-term employees to receive higher evaluations than others of equal ability
- evaluate the employee constantly throughout the year via normal job-related communication, striving for the best possible kind of evaluation—the no-surprises appraisal, when evaluator and employee know exactly where they stand with each other before the appraisal is discussed

CRITICAL SHARED KNOWLEDGE

Whether a given employee's appraisal consists almost totally of objectively measurable standards or completely of subjectively assessed criteria, it is important that this knowledge be available at the outset of the process. If objective measurements are to be applied, the employee should know in advance:

- what quantity of output (or other measure) is expected
- how much variation in output is allowable (in other words, what constitutes having met a standard or fallen short or exceeded the standard)

If subjective assessments are to be applied (for example, the evaluator's assessment of "professional manner") the employee should be given the same guidelines for judging such criteria that the evaluator will use.

In short, for any performance appraisal system to achieve fairness and to work as intended, every employee must know completely the basis on which he or she will be judged. This means that the employee must be fully knowledge-able of the measures of performance by which he or she will be evaluated.

NOTES

1. Martin G. Friedman, "10 Steps to Objective Appraisals," *Personnel Journal*, vol. 65, no. 6 (June 1986) p. 67.

2. Richard Gerard, "Is There a Need for Performance Appraisals?" *Personnel Journal*, vol. 67, no. 8 (August 1988) p. 89.

3. Sanford L. Bordman and Gerald Melnick, "Keep Productivity Ratings Timely," *Personnel Journal*, vol. 69, no.3 (March 1990) p. 50.

4. William Weitzel, "How to Improve Performance Through Successful Appraisals," *Personnel,* vol. 64, no. 10 (October 1987) p. 21.

5. Martin G. Friedman, "10 Steps to Successful Appraisals," *Personnel Journal*, vol. 65, no. 6 (June 1986) p. 67.

6. Robert G. Pajer, "Performance Appraisal: A New Era for Federal Government Managers," *Personnel Administrator*, vol. 29, no. 3 (March 1984) p. 88.

13

The Requirements of an Effective Appraisal System

IN SEARCH OF SYSTEM SUCCESS

For a performance appraisal system to have a realistic chance of being truly effective, it must satisfy a number of conditions. If it does not meet these conditions it will inevitably accomplish less than it is intended to accomplish. However, even if the system does meet all the conditions, success is not necessarily guaranteed. To become fully effective an appraisal system requires thorough, conscientious application by managers who believe in the value of performance appraisal. Careless or indifferent application can kill even the best systems or turn them into mere paper exercises. Under some circumstances a poorly implemented appraisal system can be more damaging than no system at all.

Though not all are cast in concrete concerning every approach to performance appraisal, the following are generally the factors that must receive conscientious attention if an appraisal system is to succeed.

System Objectives

The appraisal system should be designed to serve the primary objectives of performance appraisal. That is, the system should be used primarily to maintain or improve performance in the job the employee presently holds and to enhance employee development (see Chapter 1).

There are legitimate secondary objectives of appraisal, or at least additional uses of appraisal. For example, many appraisal systems are used in support of salary administration, especially in the operation of pay-for-performance schemes that apportion increases according to appraisal score. However, if the system is designed around these secondary objectives it is likely that it will not serve its primary objectives adequately and completely. This is not to say that a system that fully serves appraisal's primary objectives cannot be used for salary administration as well. A well-designed system can be put to a number of valuable secondary uses, but if secondary uses drive the system's design then it is likely that it will be less than fully effective in its principal application.

The success of even the best of systems is dependent on the people who apply it and the people to whom it is applied. The system should be designed to fit the employees and their unique needs for performance feedback and development. This suggests that the appraisal system that properly serves appraisal's objectives for one group of employees may not do so for all groups. Therefore, fully serving appraisal's objectives in the organization may require multiple appraisal systems; for example, there might legitimately be different appraisal systems for managers and rank-and-file employees or different appraisal systems for professionals and nonprofessionals. It may indeed require multiple systems to serve appraisal's objectives equally well for all employees.

System Focus

In assessing performance the system should focus on performance. Much was said in earlier chapters about avoiding the assessment of personality characteristics. However, in concentrating on performance—on the results of the employee's behavior—the system must be structured so as to also guide the user away from assessing other nonperformance elements present in any particular employee's case. For example:

- An employee's background and qualifications can inappropriately influence an evaluation by creating expectations of certain levels of performance.
- An employee's position likewise can influence expectations that in turn become self-fulfilling through appraisal scoring. The higher the perceived level of a particular department or group, the higher the group's average score tends to be. And in most organizations it can be shown that managers' scores tend to average higher than nonmanagers' scores.
- Employee potential can also influence appraisal scoring. There is a tendency for managers to give higher scores to those employees who strike them as most capable of accomplishing more and "going farther" than most other employees.

A well-designed system that uses precise evaluation criteria derived directly from employees' job descriptions will constantly encourage users to focus on actual performance to the exclusion of other factors.

Appropriateness of Criteria

The evaluation criteria, that is, the requirements on which one is evaluated, must relate as closely as possible to the kind of work being evaluated. A job description or job specification should be specific to the job that will be evaluated; never should it be simply generic to the occupation. For example, all registered nurses cannot be evaluated appropriately using a generic registered nurse job specification. Many of the nursing positions in an organization might be similar to each other but they will not be identical in enough dimensions to allow them to be treated identically.

Management Support

The performance appraisal system must receive genuine top management support. This must be sincere, visible, active support—not simply lip service to the supposed value of appraisal.

Unfortunately, many organizations' systems enjoy only passive support and often only the tolerance of the top managers. It is likely that many top managers do not know how their own appraisal systems operate in detail, and that most of these same top managers never perform an evaluation.

It is also a function of top management to supply the resources consumed by an appraisal system, the money needed for forms and materials, the time required for employee meetings, evaluator training, and system administration, and computer resources as necessary. Appraisal is receiving far less than its due if management's attitude is that appraisal is "free," generally something that's accomplished by squeezing it in with all other tasks.

Management also must be committed to the use of appraisal for all of its intended purposes, especially as concerns employee development. Few conditions can be more demoralizing than those that exist when employees learn of their capacity for promotion and growth through performance appraisal and yet see the best promotional opportunities filled from outside of the organization.

Employee Acceptance

The most successful appraisal systems are those that have achieved a high level of acceptance by those who are evaluated. Employee acceptance results in part from fair and impartial appraisal that always occurs on time (when it is expected to occur). Acceptance comes also with employee involvement, which can occur in a number of ways at several points: employee participation in developing or revising job descriptions and in writing evaluation criteria and developing standards, participation through optional self-appraisal, and active participation in determining goals and targets and plans for improvement.

Generally the most comfortable level of employee acceptance exists when employees and evaluators alike hold similar positive expectations of the appraisal system.

Standards of Performance

For all criteria stemming from an individual's job description there should be either objective measures of output or clear choices that describe actual performance relative to what is expected. That is, all expected performance should be expressed as simple targets or standards.

Recall the description of a true standard offered in the opening section of Chapter 12 as consisting, precisely as a true objective does, of what must be done, how much should be done, and when it must be done. Although always there, the *when* is often present by implication only; the *what* is stated as the evaluation criteria; and the *how much* exists as the expectation. The *how much* is often referred to alone as the standard, yet it is the three parts together that the employee needs to know.

In any effective appraisal system the standards of performance are made known to the employee. In other words, it is a requirement of an effective appraisal system that each employee know in advance the expectations against which he or she will be evaluated.

Evaluator Education

All evaluators require basic and continuing education in how to apply the appraisal system. It is insufficient simply to allow evaluators to learn how to use the system by reading a manual or by utilizing audio or video tape materials. Basic in-person education is required, including individual coaching from time to time. Just as important is regular refresher education in which evaluators again cover what many of them doubtless think they already know well. And as much as possible of this education, refresher as well as initial, should take place in a group setting.

One of the greatest areas of chronic difficulty with appraisal systems is inconsistency of application from one evaluator to another. The more that the evaluators in the organization receive their training in a group setting, the higher the level of appraisal consistency that will be experienced throughout the organization.

The Appraisal Interview

All that is said about the appraisal interview in Chapter 7 is pertinent here. It matters little to write a thorough, insightful appraisal if it is not discussed with the employee—and on time. Often to the employee the appraisal interview is the appraisal; without the interview, appraisal is a hollow paper exercise.

Employee performance often represents an area of difference between employee and manager and frequently is a source of interpersonal conflict. The performance appraisal interview is a potentially strong channel of communication between manager and employee in this area of difference. Therefore it should be an object of the appraisal interview to communicate more clearly, and more readily, and thus reduce the potential for interpersonal conflict.

System Administration

Even the best of appraisal systems can fail in the absence of conscientious system administration. As important as employee performance appraisal may be, most of the time it ranks well below patient care and other operating concerns on the relative scale of priorities. An evaluator who has the best of intentions can miss an appraisal's due date in the normal course of business; likewise a busy evaluator can let a seemingly routine appraisal interview slide or might forget to send a few personnel file copies of appraisals to the human resource department. Necessary activities and deadlines understandably can be missed unless someone exercises responsibility for keeping the system moving.

Job descriptions, job specifications, and performance standards all have to be kept up to date. Forms have to be ordered and stocked and, depending on the system, perhaps supplied with employee information and furnished to evaluators with schedules for completion. Delinquencies have to be followed up. File copies have to be put into personnel records. Evaluators have to be trained and retrained, and employees' questions need to be answered. Perhaps even employees' objections to some parts of the appraisal process have to be dealt with through some sort of appeal or grievance process. Without these activities taking place on a timely basis, the operation of an otherwise effective performance appraisal system can come to a standstill.

System administration is best accomplished centrally, usually by the human resource department (with, of course, the acknowledged backing of top management).

A Working Tool

Once the appraisal is accomplished and the interview is concluded, the appraisal form is filed—but the appraisal best not be forgotten. The days of file-it-and-forget-it appraisals should be well behind us; the appraisal should be at least as much of a plan for the immediate future as it is a recounting of the immediate past. The appraisal must be a working tool for the weeks and months to come.

If a given appraisal involves joint target setting, management by objectives, or any other participatory activity, it cannot readily be left out of sight and mind (see Chapter 15). Targets and objectives ordinarily involve time spans and deadlines; time spans and deadlines mean periodic follow up.

An effective appraisal system will encourage regular monitoring of performance against the most recent appraisal. If performance seems to be declining, the manager should know this and be dealing with it long before the next appraisal; if performance is consistent or even improving, the manager should know this and acknowledge it with the employee.

In short, an effective performance appraisal is not a snapshot of performance at a point in time, and it is not just a summary of performance at the end of a period of time. Rather, an effective performance appraisal is a starting point for future improvement.

FOR EFFECTIVE PERFORMANCE APPRAISAL

In summary, an effective performance appraisal system:

1. is specifically designed to serve the primary objectives of performance appraisal
2. focuses on performance to the total exclusion of personality
3. evaluates performance using criteria based completely on current job descriptions
4. receives visible, active top management support
5. enjoys the acceptance of the majority of employees
6. utilizes standards of performance known to the employees in advance of evaluation
7. includes initial and regular refresher education of evaluators
8. requires the completion of an appraisal interview with every evaluation
9. is administered conscientiously with all steps occurring in timely fashion
10. produces an evaluation that is a working tool for continuing improvement in work performance

HELPFUL—BUT NOT ESSENTIAL

As far as it is possible to do so, the completed performance appraisal form should comprise a self-contained record, one that can be taken from an employee's personnel file and read and understood completely without reference to other documents. It should not be necessary to have to cross-reference an appraisal manual, evaluation key, or list of explanations to determine what any particular rating means.

This is not sufficiently compelling as to be considered an absolute require-ment. The ability to completely interpret an appraisal without other information is largely a matter of convenience. However, utilizing an appraisal system built in the manner described in the last few chapters makes it possible for many appraisals to consist of only two or three pages: the appraisal form and the job specification, complete with standards and the meaning of the scores.

Exceptions occur in some systems given the manner in which some direct-care functions have adopted criteria-based appraisal. In some instances the detailed criteria and their assessment require eight, ten, or a dozen sheets, so the tendency is to place the appraisal form alone in the personnel file and retain the back up elsewhere (for example, in nursing department files).

Part IV
Other Appraisal Considerations

14

Different Faces
of Appraisal

TYPES OF APPRAISAL APPROACHES

The overwhelming majority of performance appraisal systems past and present are of the kind known as rating scale approaches. Rating scales are far and away the most numerous and popular appraisal mechanisms. Rating scale systems include the good and the bad, the successful and the failed. They include the old personality-based methods as well as the presently recommended criteria-based methods. Up to this point, this book has been entirely about rating scale appraisal methods.

A rating scale system is simply a system with which evaluators use some sort of a scale to assess a number of characteristics, requirements, or criteria. Whether it is a progression of eight or ten subjective assessments ranging from "poor" to "outstanding" or a simple choice between "yes" or "no" or among "failed to meet standard," "met standard," or "exceeded standard," a rating scale is essentially the measuring stick used to appraise performance. It is also the horizontal scale so frequently referred to in earlier chapters.

Performance appraisal essentially began with rating scales, and although there have been some occasional forays into other approaches, it is rating scales that command the most attention as appraisal systems continue to be refined and improved.

Some users of performance appraisal have developed or adopted approaches other than rating scales in attempts to remove judgment from the appraisal process. In the extreme we encounter the occasional system that is so encumbered with measures, countermeasures, checks, and cross checks that appraisal seems to become a matter of scaling, weighting, and calculating. However, it is not possible to completely remove judgment from performance appraisal, and the system designer who seeks to do so will be disappointed. As long as appraisal involves humans making assessments or choices, judgment will be present.

While some have tried to eliminate judgment altogether, others have attempted to rely on gross judgments that assume the evaluator knows all and sees all, or on the net judgmental impact of multiple evaluators.

In correctly altering working appraisal systems over the years, there appears to have been a two-fold treatment of judgment. First, judgment of the person has been totally removed in favor of judgment of the person's performance. Second, subsequent efforts have concentrated on reducing and refining the judgment of performance so that the final evaluation includes the net impact of some objective measures plus a number of specific, narrowly defined judgments.

In addition to rating scales a number of other approaches have surfaced now and then and are still found in occasional use in certain environments. These other approaches include:

- methods of employee comparison, consisting primarily of two variations—employee ranking, and the forced distribution method
- checklist approaches of either of two variations, the weighted checklist method and the forced choice method
- the critical incident method
- the field review approach
- freeform essay appraisal
- group appraisal methods, including both multiple supervisor and peer group processes
- electronic performance monitoring, which is not a true method of appraisal but which deserves discussion because of the growing use of computers in performing work

Rating Scale Variations

As demonstrated in many of the preceding chapters, the rating scale approach may take many appearances. However, all rating scales are essentially of two kinds—continuous or discrete. Using the continuous scale form, for a particular criterion or characteristic the evaluator simply places a mark somewhere along a continuous line to represent the value of the rating. Figure 14–1 is an example of a continuous rating scale for a single performance criterion.

A discrete scale contains a number of specific choices from which the evaluator must choose in describing performance against a particular criterion or characteristic. These choices are usually arrayed from poorest to best performance, or vice versa. Figure 14–2 is an example of a discrete rating scale for a single performance criterion.

Rating scales are easy to understand, and once one has the grasp of a system's operations they are easy to use. Rating scales also readily permit statistical analysis of scores through the ability to readily determine measures of cen-

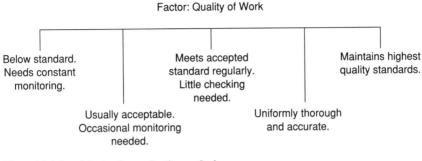

Figure 14–1 One Criterion from a Continuous Scale

tral tendency, skewness, and dispersion, so they facilitate ready comparison of scores among employees.

However, there are drawbacks to rating scales. There is the frequently encountered impression that high scores on some criteria can compensate for low scores on others. Unless the particular system is designed to highlight substandard scores on individual criteria, there is a chance of genuine performance problems being masked by scores that are satisfactory overall. This is complicated by the fact that in practice the evaluations done using rating scales tend to cluster on the high side.

There are frequently rating scale problems with words and their meanings. Consider the simple five-level rating scale of Table 14–1. With even as few words as are used in conjunction with this scale, there are opportunities for misunderstanding and disagreement. In number 2, for example, what is "essentially?" How does "essentially" meeting job requirements really differ from fully meeting job requirements? Is it 98 percent? Is it 90 percent? How much leeway does it include? Or in number 4, how does one meet job requirements "with distinction," and how does this differ from "fully" meeting them? And is it not likely that some will fail to see the difference between meeting requirements with distinction and exceeding requirements?

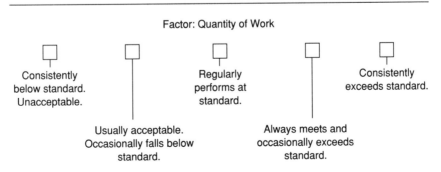

Figure 14–2 One Criterion from a Discrete Scale

Table 14–1 Five-Point Rating Scale

1. Fails to meet job requirements.
2. Essentially meets job requirements.
3. Fully meets job requirements.
4. Meets job requirements with distinction.
5. Exceeds all job requirements.

We cannot expect to remove all of the subjectivity from all non-numerical performance descriptors, but the more nonspecific words are used—words like adequate, sufficient, normally, satisfactory, and such—the more the resulting ratings will be subject to varying interpretations.

One further variation on rating scales deserves mention: behaviorally anchored rating scales (BARS). Figure 14–3 is an example of such a scale for a single evaluation criterion. Dating back to the early to middle 1960s, BARS represented a major step away from the assessment of personality. This kind of scale relates well to performance criteria that must be assessed subjectively, such as, in the example of Figure 14–3, the criteria a middle manager might use in evaluating a supervisor.

Using BARS, a scale is created for each major component or task area of the position. Each scale ties sample kinds of behavior associated with a job description task to an overall description of task performance. Although there may be perhaps six, seven, or eight levels of performance described and some fairly broad judgments are required, this process nevertheless steers the evaluator away from personality effects and focuses attention on behavior or actions.

Employee Comparison

The simplest means of employee comparison, employee ranking, is exactly what its name suggests: the evaluator ranks his or her subordinates on an overall basis according to job performance and value to the organization. This process is simple to apply. Approached in the easiest manner, the evaluator can simply designate the best and poorest performers first, then select the best and poorest of the remainder, and so on until all in the group have been placed in order.

Some will argue that employee ranking is a satisfactory method in a small group all members of which the supervisor knows equally well. However, this method is highly subject to personal bias; there is a tendency to place employees in rank order based at least partly on how well they are liked.

Some ranking plans expect the evaluator to place employees in groups such as the lowest third, middle third, and top third, suggesting a relationship with

Position: Manager

Job Characteristic: Delegation

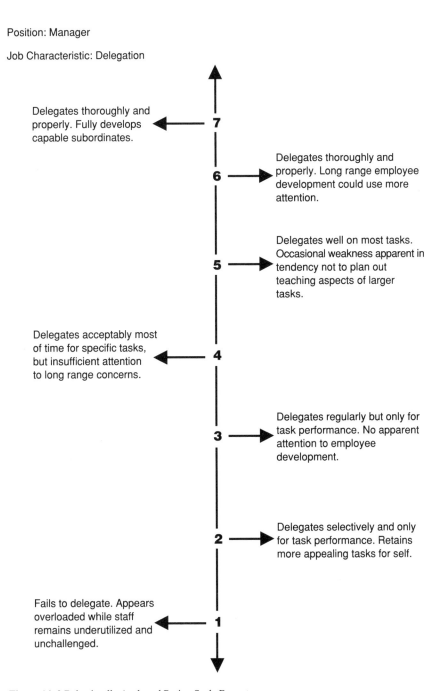

Delegates thoroughly and properly. Fully develops capable subordinates.

7

6 Delegates thoroughly and properly. Long range employee development could use more attention.

5 Delegates well on most tasks. Occasional weakness apparent in tendency not to plan out teaching aspects of larger tasks.

Delegates acceptably most of time for specific tasks, but insufficient attention to long range concerns.

4

3 Delegates regularly but only for task performance. No apparent attention to employee development.

2 Delegates selectively and only for task performance. Retains more appealing tasks for self.

Fails to delegate. Appears overloaded while staff remains underutilized and unchallenged.

1

Figure 14–3 Behaviorally Anchored Rating Scale Format

below average, average, and above average. This process, however simple, usually fails to match the reality of performance by members of the work group.

Some rating scale systems that called for placing people at points along a scale according to apparent value led to the clustering of employees at particular points on the scale, usually near the high end. To prevent this clustering the forced distribution method was designed. Under this approach the evaluator must allocate, for example, 10 percent to the top end of the scale, 20 percent to the second highest group, 40 percent to the middle area, 20 percent to the next lowest group, and 10 percent to the lowest group.

The objective of forced distribution is to spread out the rating according to a so-called normal distribution (the well-known bell-shaped curve). This method possesses numerous shortcomings. In a business organization the evaluator should be dealing with a select group of people, with those who cannot or will not do the work being weeded out along the way through probationary employment periods and the like. The distribution of abilities and performance in a typical work group should be decidedly skewed, with the so-called average performers clustered somewhat near the bottom, but with substandard performers being few in number at any given time.

Checklists

Checklist evaluation systems require a great deal of development effort.

The weighted checklist is made up of a large number of statements describing types of behavior associated with a specific job or family of related jobs. The descriptions cover a number of variations in the appropriateness of the behavior in fulfilling the requirements of the job. There is a value or weight associated with every statement, and when rating an employee the evaluator checks all of the statements that most accurately describe the person's behavior. A total score is developed by averaging the weights of all of the statements selected by the appraiser. The actual weights of the statements are kept secret from the evaluator, supposedly so that it is not possible to deliberately make a score come out as desired.

A sample set of statements from the evaluation of a supervisor appears as Exhibit 14–1. The evaluator must indicate whether each statement is most or least descriptive of the person's performance. Note that although A and B both seem favorable to the person being evaluated, only B differentiates between high and low performance supervisors. Items C and E appear generally unfavorable, and D is relatively neutral.

In addition to the fact that it requires a great deal of work to establish and implement this method, the business of utilizing secret weights, known and applied only in the personnel department, at least partially alienates many

Exhibit 14–1 Sample Statements: Weighted Checklist

Most	*Least*	
A	A	Seldom makes mistakes.
B	B	Is respected by subordinates.
C	C	Does not completely follow through on assignments.
D	D	Feels that own position is more important than other jobs.
E	E	Does not express views and opinions with any degree of self confidence.

evaluators who feel that they are being treated as less than fully responsible supervisors. And it does seem as though the practice of hiding some important system elements from anyone, whether evaluator or employee, could be a significant drawback.

There are other, and quite similar, variations on the checklist approach. Some of these utilize weights, some do not, and some, like the forced choice method, require the evaluator to make a selection for all statements even though some may not seem to be appropriate for inclusion.

Critical Incident

Critical incidents are those events that occur during the evaluation period when the employee either makes an outstanding contribution or suffers a significant failure when trying to fulfill an important job responsibility. For each critical incident there should be no doubt that the event was the direct result of the employee's behavior.[1] As the evaluation period proceeds the evaluator simply records in a notebook or on a simple form all such important positive and negative instances of performance.

Using the critical incident method the appraiser must be careful to describe performance exclusively, avoiding all temptation to assign cause to the behavior that produced the incidents. The tendency to second-guess cause is especially likely to arise around negative incidents.

The primary advantage of this method is that a clear track of performance is being created while the information is current. Also, the evaluator is always capturing the essentials of evaluation; even in other appraisal approaches this is generally the way the evaluators who keep anecdotal notes track performance over the evaluation period.

The drawbacks of this approach have been enough to severely hamper its general use. Many evaluators do not like to write, and more than a few do not write well. Procrastination is common; it is all too easy to put off writing something until there is more time, and many incidents get written up incorrectly or not at all. There is also the danger of going too far in recording incidents and creating the impression with employees that everything they do gets written up.

Field Review

The most appealing feature of this approach, at least to the evaluators, is that the evaluators fill out no forms and do very little paperwork at all. The department supervisor is interviewed by a personnel department interviewer to obtain all pertinent information on each employee. The personnel representative writes up a detailed appraisal following whatever format the organization uses and submits this to the supervisor for modifications or suggestions. Overall ratings only are used; there are no degrees, factors, or incremental scores as such.

On the positive side, field review relieves the supervisor of paperwork and greatly reduces what to some evaluators is the agony of appraisal. It also ensures that appraisal will be given adequate attention and that reviews are done on time because the personnel department essentially controls the process.

The negatives concerning field review are enough to prevent its use in nearly all business organizations. The process consumes the time of two management representatives, the supervisor and the personnel representative. Since it discourages writing, supervisors are denied what they need to improve as writers— active writing practice. The primary drawback, however, is financial; it requires much more personnel staff. A medium size health care institution would have to add several personnel interviewers to its staff to accomplish field review for everyone.

Essay

The essay method is essentially the same as the field review method but with all of the thinking, writing, correcting, and so on done by the evaluator. No specific form is used, although the evaluator is usually provided with some general questions to answer about the employee or an outline to follow. The evaluator simply describes performance—good and bad points, perhaps critical incidents, apparent training needs, and perhaps potential. In the absence of a pattern or outline it is best to group the comments under headings such as task performance, apparent strengths, training needs, etc.

On the positive side this method is versatile and requires no specific forms. On the negative side it remains totally up to the appraiser to keep all remarks job related. This method is also difficult for evaluators who do not write well or who do not like writing, and it is tough to achieve consistency across departments with this approach.

The essay form of appraisal works best for relatively small groups of educated, self-governing professionals, especially if all such people report to a single manager. This method can work well, for example, in evaluating a small group of management consultants or public accountants.

Group Appraisal Methods

Two forms of performance appraisal occasionally encountered involve evaluation by groups of people, one using groups of supervisors and one employing groups of employees' peers.

Supervisory group appraisal emphasizes the growth and development of the individual. Conclusions about performance and decisions having to do with pay increases and promotions and such are usually made by the immediate supervisor in consultation with other supervisors. The appraisal group is usually made up of the employee's immediate supervisor plus three or four other supervisors who have knowledge of the employee's work performance.

This method is ordinarily quite thorough, and the use of multiple judges usually moderates any bias that might be present in the immediate supervisor's assessment. However, since the process involves several people there is a severe limitation in the large amount of time consumed, and also most employees are not sufficiently well known by three or four other supervisors for this approach to be applied successfully.

Peer group appraisal often appears under the label of team appraisal, since it is frequently utilized with employees who work as a team.

A team is a group of individuals working together in such a way that the success of any individual depends on the success of the group. Whether quantitative or narrative, participative or autocratic, individual performance appraisals do not contribute to team building because they ordinarily do not address the effect of the group on the individual or vice versa.[2]

This process of having the members of a team evaluate each other is most useful as a supplement to regular supervisory appraisal, and not in place of it. This approach is extremely valuable in revealing differences in group members' perceptions of each other. It is best to utilize strict criteria-based appraisal when peer groups are involved; personal likes and dislikes vary considerably in any group and peer group appraisal is highly subject to personal biases. All persons in a peer appraisal group must use exactly the same job-based criteria, plus perhaps additional special criteria based on each individual's team role.

Team or peer appraisal may be increasingly helpful in the immediate future. Today's new organizational structures in which decentralization has given managers much more to oversee have created conditions under which a single manager cannot possibly be fully knowledgeable of the capabilities and performance of a large number of people. New organizational designs, such as spans of supervision of 60 people or more, make multiple raters necessary for the flat organization of the future.[3]

Although a peer group appraisal is done by all members of the group together, the appraisal interview should still be a traditional one-on-one conducted by the immediate supervisor. The supervisor, however, is presenting not just his or her own evaluation, but rather is presenting a consensus rating developed by the group. All members of a given group should be evaluated by the others—not just some of them.

Peer group appraisal, of course, takes a far greater total amount of time than individual appraisal. Also, it is easy to disturb some people's sensitivities in this process; it helps to be a bit thick skinned in the face of criticism representing the consensus of several people who are co-workers and perhaps friends. This is mitigated somewhat when ratings are kept anonymous within the group.

Properly done, peer group appraisal has some strong advantages and produces good, valuable appraisals. More often than not an employee's peers are most knowledgeable about the work to be judged and about the employee's performance and behavior. Peers also usually know how the specific employee acts when higher management is not present.

Electronic Performance Monitoring

It is estimated that by the year 2000 as many as 30 million visual display terminal users might have their performance monitored by electronic methods.[4]

Computer performance monitoring can be extremely simple. The process uses predetermined targets to rate the employee. Using a standard that has been developed carefully to allow for an average amount of normal delay and operator personal time, the computer simply counts the number of times each standardized task is performed. Electronic performance monitoring sets very explicit standards accompanied by expectations that are incorporated into daily work routines.[5] Further, proponents point out that since all output is measured against a standard by machine, there is no opportunity for fallible human judgment and absolutely no chance of rating bias due to personality effects.

The process sounds simple enough; however, electronic performance monitoring already has become an employee relations minefield. Unions and other labor representatives generally see monitoring as an insidious management practice and a blatant invasion of privacy, while a number of employers see it as a positive tool for managing workloads and gauging employee performance.[6]

Some who sanction the use of electronic monitoring point out that it is nothing really new, but rather is simply one form of electronic surveillance. Among the other forms is telephone monitoring, which enables employers to find out whether customer service employees handle calls efficiently and courteously. Opponents of monitoring have described it as, among other undesirable characterizations, "the mental bludgeoning of an ever-vigilant Big Brother" under which "employees are called to account for such extraneous subjects as the frequency and duration of washroom visits."[7]

Some of the more recent—and either unanswered, or insufficiently answered—questions arising about electronic performance monitoring include:

- Can monitored employees working in states where privacy laws entitle them to see their personnel files also successfully demand to see their complete monitoring results?
- If personal information collected via monitoring is revealed in a way that causes harm, can employees sue for public disclosure of private facts?
- Can employees pursue charges through the National Labor Relations Board (NLRB) if monitoring appears to be used to identify or punish union activity?
- Can employees fired as a result of monitoring successfully claim breach of contract and good faith?[8]

The controversy surrounding electronic performance monitoring is not likely to be resolved easily or at any time in the foreseeable future. In any case, even if acceptable to employees, monitoring provides only a physical count of tasks or transactions completed and perhaps a record of error rate (a quality indicator). Few people, even those who spend the entire work day at a computer keyboard, can be fully and fairly evaluated electronically. No matter how automated, every job has its own unique requirements for human interaction and its own opportunities for innovation and creativity—and these and other performance-related factors can be assessed fairly only through the intervention of supervisory judgment.

RATING SCALES AND PRECAUTIONS

Although they may range from outmoded and inappropriate personality assessment to the latest in criteria- and standards-based appraisal, the majority of performance appraisal systems in use are variations on the rating scale approach. Some of the other approaches described in this chapter have legitimate, if fairly narrow, uses, and some, notably team or peer group appraisal, serve as useful supplements to rating scale systems.

Regardless of the particular approach or combination of approaches used, however, a couple of major precautions are in order.

Average Is Only Average

Average is just that, average—the mean value of multiple values. Mathematically, average is the center of a given population; it is found at the central point—the high point—of the well known and dramatically misunderstood bell-shaped curve (known in statistical terminology as the normal distribution).

A great many users of appraisal systems mistakenly regard average performance as the normal expectation of management and in this manner equate average performance with standard performance. However, standard performance or working at standard describes the work of someone who is meeting the requirements of the job, and anything less than this standard performance requires action to improve that performance or, if that cannot be accomplished, to remove the person from the work group. Mistakenly equating average and standard incorrectly labels the normal distribution and suggests that half of the organization's employees are performing at substandard levels (see Figure 14-4).

Employee performance well may be described by the normal distribution, but labeled properly (as in Figure 14–5) the "average" is the true mathematical average of performance scores and "standard" is that minimal acceptable level

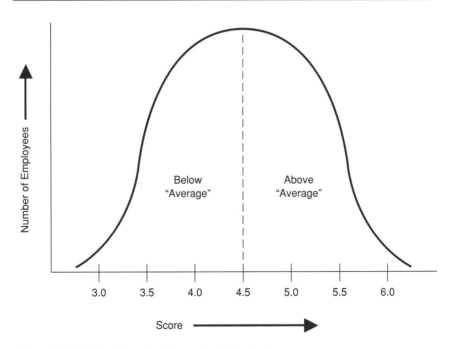

Figure 14–4 Mistakenly Equating "Average" and "Standard"

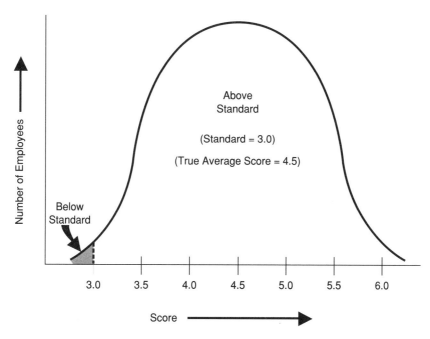

Figure 14–5 "Average" in Proper Relationship to "Standard"

of performance that employees must exhibit to remain employed. With the exception of a few below-standard scores, most appraisal scores range from standard on upward. Therefore the true average score is always higher than the standard.

There are also some problems of language and perception having to do with the use of "average." Referring again to Figure 14-5, consider that most employees who score 4.5 in this particular appraisal system would not object, and may even display pleasure, at hearing their performance described as well above standard. However, many of these same employees may display noticeable displeasure at hearing their performance described as average. Not a great many people like to hear themselves described as average ("What, me? Only average?").

THE CRITICAL VARIABLE IN THE SYSTEM

The critical variable in any performance appraisal system is the human being. Starting with those who develop the system and the top managers who need to support it, and extending down to the rank-and-file employees who either accept or resist performance appraisal, no appraisal system is any better than the people who are involved in it.

The key people in performance appraisal are, of course, the evaluators. The managers who apply the system can make or break it, and ultimately no system, no matter how well constructed, can guarantee appropriate behavior by managers who probably should not be managers.

NOTES

1. John Lawrie, "Prepare for a Performance Appraisal," *Personnel Journal*, vol. 69, no. 4 (April 1990) p. 132.

2. Peggy Lanza, "Team Appraisals," *Personnel Journal*, vol. 64, no. 3 (March 1985) p. 47.

3. Mark R. Edwards, "A Joint Effort Leads to Accurate Appraisals," *Personnel Journal*, vol. 69, no.6 (June 1990) p. 122.

4. N. Faye Angel, "Evaluating Employees by Computer," *Personnel Administrator*, vol. 34, no. 11 (November 1989) p. 67.

5. *Ibid*, p. 68.

6. The Bureau of National Affairs, "VDTs in the Workplace: New Issues, New Answers, Second Edition, A BNA Special Report," *Labor Relations Week* (July 29, 1987) pp. 23–24.

7. *Ibid,* p. 24.

8. The Bureau of National Affairs, "VDTs in the 1990s: Advancing Technologies, Mounting Concerns," *Labor Relations Week, Special Supplement* (August 1, 1990) p. 12.

15

Goal Setting in
Performance Appraisal

EMPLOYEE INVOLVEMENT

In recent years we have been told repeatedly of the need for employee involvement in activities that once were considered the sole province of management. Performance appraisal is one such activity; in earlier days an appraisal was usually a one-way rendering of an individual's perceived personality, capability, and performance. Today performance appraisal is recognized as one of the management tasks for which a degree of employee involvement can enhance results for employee and evaluator alike.

There are a number of opportunities for employee involvement in aspects of performance appraisal or activities directly related to performance appraisal. These include:

- active participation in writing or revising an employee's own job description
- employee participation in creating evaluation criteria and developing measurement standards
- active participation in the performance appraisal interview, including the opportunity to append comments to an appraisal and to protest ratings that the employee does not agree with
- the opportunity to conduct a self-appraisal (at the employee's option) and bring this into the total appraisal process
- the frequently available opportunity to utilize goal-, target-, or objective-setting processes in conjunction with or in support of performance appraisal.

Not all of the foregoing involvement opportunities are pertinent to all levels and classes of employees. However, at least one and perhaps more of these opportunities for involvement can be extended to every employee in the organization.

All opportunities for employee involvement, and all of the manager's efforts to involve employees in the form, direction, and quality of their performance appraisals, should have the desired effect of encouraging the employees to own a piece of the process and thus to accept responsibility for their own performance and their own progress. There are few if any other activities that can produce this effect better than the use of goals, targets, or objectives.

GOALS, TARGETS, AND OBJECTIVES

In the general literature of performance appraisal the terms *goal, target,* and *objective* are used essentially interchangeably. They are applied similarly in this discussion. It is important to keep this similarity of terms in mind; in certain other areas of management interest, notably long-range planning, one can find distinct differences among these terms. In some of the planning literature, for example, differing definitions are given for goal and objective. However, every normal dictionary and thesaurus lists goal and objective as synonyms for each other.

A true goal (or objective or target) must always consist of three parts:

- what is to be done
- how much is to be done
- when it is to be done

The most common weakness in all processes that involve the use of goals or objectives is that all of the above three elements are not present. The *what* is, of course, always there. However, the *how much* is too often vague and the *when*, the weakest part of most so-called goals, is frequently missing.

The employee who states as a goal, "To improve my attendance," or the supervisor who states, "To reduce my department's supply expense," has stated only *what*, yet goal statements of this form are common. Putting the supervisor's statement in true goal or objective form would produce something like: "To reduce my department's supply expense (what) by 10 percent (how much) within six months (when)." Occasionally the how much and when will be implied; sometimes the how much is obvious (all of it, whatever it is) and sometimes the way an objective is written in conjunction with an appraisal makes it plain that the *when* is the next scheduled appraisal. But whether directly stated or implied, the three elements—what, how much, and when—must be present for the statement to represent a true objective.

Usually Room for Objectives

It is almost always possible to include an objective or two with even the simplest of performance appraisals. This at times need be no more than a very simply stated objective, perhaps suggested by the evaluator but rounded out in discussion with the employee, introduced during the appraisal interview.

Any goal or objective used in conjunction with performance appraisal always should reflect a need for or desirability of improvement. Specifically:

- A need for improvement can apply to any employee, at any level, on the occasion of any performance appraisal in which correction of some problem is indicated. Although an employee's overall appraisal score may be at standard or better, if an agreed-on rating of one particular job description point is substandard, this level of performance on this particular job task calls for corrective action. An objective stemming from a need for improvement should be part of any performance appraisal that indicates substandard results in the performance of any part of the job.
- The desirability of improvement encompasses the broad reasons behind all objectives other than corrective objectives. It is the supposed desirability of improvement—the improvement of performance over and above standard, acceptable performance—that the broader, more formal goal-setting processes (like those discussed in the following sections) address.

Most of what is written about the use of goal-setting mechanisms in conjunction with performance appraisal addresses objectives that reflect the desirability of improvement. These objectives ordinarily should originate with the employee or should at least be products of employee and manager collaboration. Objectives aimed at further improvements in performance that is already at standard should not be dictated or mandated. This is the critical difference between objectives addressing the desirability of improvement and objectives addressing correction of substandard performance. While a manager certainly might ask for any employee's input in formulating a corrective objective, it remains the manager's province to mandate standard performance as a condition of continued employment. Therefore, corrective objectives are properly set forth as requirements of the employee.

Objectives of all forms may or may not relate to the normal appraisal cycle as their time period. If, for example, a manager gives an employee a corrective objective because of substandard performance in an important job task, the manager will want to ensure correction well before the next appraisal (probably a year away) rolls around. In this instance the manager will probably call for correction within a few weeks. (Deadlines for corrective action of 30, 60, or 90 days are fairly common.)

Some objectives' time lines can be established arbitrarily to match an appraisal cycle. However, many objectives will lend themselves to different time spans. Some will seem well served by a one-year time line; some may require more than a year. Some may lend themselves to time spans of six months, three months, or one month. Some may even require weekly review.

Overall it is best if objectives' check points vary over time. Each objective's follow up, embodying, as it will, contact between manager and employee similar to but less formal than the annual appraisal, will tend to reinforce both the manager-employee relationship and the integral role of performance appraisal in that relationship.

JOINT TARGET SETTING

A number of variations are available concerning what is to follow. However, this and other slightly different approaches are built upon a common series of events—employee and manager agree on the current contents of the job, agree on a set of targets or objectives, and decide when and how to examine results. All variations on this theme begin at the same point—the job description.

Job Description Update

Working completely independently of each other, employee and manager each thoroughly review the employee's job description and mark it up to reflect the job's present composition. (If no job description exists, each party begins by writing out the major elements of a current job description. The process proceeds in the same manner as it would if working with an existing description.)

It is important that the two parties work alone initially so that each is able to capture his or her own particular view of the job. It is not unusual to find that the employee's perception and the manager's perception of the same job differ markedly, and such differences must be thrashed out so that each thinks of the job in essentially the same way. When they each have drafted a complete job description separately, they next get together to work out any differences in their perceptions of the job.

In working out differences the manager's role should be much more that of consultant or counselor than that of boss. It should be the manager's intent in this process to ameliorate differences between the two versions of the job description by selling the employee on certain additional changes. However, the manager needs to be as completely open to the employee's view of the job as he or she would expect the employee to be to the manager's view. Employees sometimes will err in the direction of making the job sound more the way they perhaps would like it to be. The only real control the manager need exert on the process of reaching agreement is to ensure that the job remains or becomes what the organization needs it to be, rather than what the employee might prefer.

Most reasonable employees will not let their desires and preferences run away with them. The majority of employees can usually provide some valuable insight into the job that may have escaped management's attention. In most instances there is no one who knows the detailed working of a particular job better than the person who performs that job every day.

Sometimes it may take two or three iterations to arrive at complete agreement on all the significant duties of the job. Often, however, a single meeting will result in agreement. Regardless of how much or how little time it takes, however, the result of this process should be mutual understanding of all major task areas of the job and agreement on the relative importance of each.

Goals, Objectives, or Performance Targets

After agreement is reached on the job description, the employee should work alone once again to develop a tentative set of goals for the evaluation period immediately ahead. Each goal—there should be perhaps four, five, or six goals, all relating to aspects of the employee's job—should exhibit the three defining characteristics of an objective: what is to be done, how much is to be done, and by when it should be done. The time span for attainment of each goal should relate to the goal itself, not to some other concern such as the performance evaluation period. Goals typically will have differing time requirements, allowing some to be reached in less time than the lapse between appraisals, while some must take longer. The intent would be to look at each goal in its own time frame but also to look at goal attainment or progress against goals at appraisal time.

In addition to including the basic defining characteristics of goals or objectives, each goal suggested by the employee should:

- represent at least some modest improvement in how something is done, thus presenting some challenge to its attainment
- be manageable by the employee, such that the employee controls all resources necessary to the goal's attainment (that is, the employee does not have to depend on someone else to do something before the goal can be reached)
- be practical and realistic; that is, be doable in the chosen time period using normally available means

The employee's target plan or set of goals also can include one or two personal goals, if the manager so agrees, especially if these are oriented toward improving the employee's job-related knowledge or capability.

Again employee and manager meet in something of a negotiating mode, reviewing the employee's target plan in detail and striving to achieve agreement on this plan. Once again, if at all possible the manager's role should remain one of consultant or counselor, advising and explaining as may be needed. The manager should consider a stronger approach only if in spite of all good counsel the employee insists on goals that are clearly unreasonable or that are obviously inconsistent with organizational objectives.

The employee and manager are negotiating what has to be accomplished in the time before the next performance appraisal review. At all times goals must be specific, measurable, time bound, and challenging. They also must be in sync with the goals of other employees and the goals of the department.[1]

As this stage is brought to a close the employee and manager should agree when to get together to check progress and evaluate accomplishments, both specifically for each objective and generally for the plan as a whole.

Meeting to Review Results

The manager and employee should discuss job performance periodically. The subordinate should bring in action plans for approval, recommend corrective action for problem resolution, and offer ideas and suggestions for improving individual and departmental performance.[2] In actuality a target-plan-related meeting between employee and manager can be:

- a status report or progress review concerning one or more goals
- a problem-solving session, in which two minds are brought to bear on a problem of concern to both
- a planning session in which goals, time lines, or both are revised to reflect current information, or in which new goals are developed
- a performance appraisal interview, or a significant part of one

Benefits of Joint Target Setting

Both employee and manager stand to gain from joint target setting. The benefits of this process include:

- A current job description results from the joint effort, specifically one that the manager and employee are in complete agreement on
- The employee knows well in advance the criteria relative to performance appraisal on which he or she will be evaluated, thus satisfying one of the fundamental requirements of an effective appraisal system
- The employee is strengthened in planning and in problem solving

- The employee and manager are brought together on items of mutual importance, thus strengthening the manager-employee relationship
- Both gain the knowledge that simply hitting a target is not nearly as important as the total process of approaching problems, setting targets, analyzing changes, and replanning.

MANAGEMENT BY OBJECTIVES

The process of joint target setting just described, and for that matter all of its variations, embody the key elements of the well-known (at least by name) technique of management by objectives (MBO). These key elements concern the employee's development and pursuit of a plan of goals, targets, or objectives that are consistent with the organization's objectives and that represent improved performance in the employee's area of responsibility. Frequently MBO is seen as applying largely to managerial employees, and many corporate MBO programs limit its use to just managers, but it is equally applicable—as is any of the joint target-setting approaches—to most nonmanagerial employees as well.

Management by objectives has been so well known, so talked about and referred to in the literature of management, that it may be surprising to learn that its principles are simple and its key elements are few. Yet these principles and elements have been viewed and reviewed from so many perspectives as to suggest that so much attention must indicate that much remains to be considered about MBO. A 1981 bibliography on the subject of MBO, well over a decade old as of this writing, listed 81 books and 1,270 articles written about management by objectives.[3] All of this still-growing collection of words has its origins in a single chapter of one book published in 1954, Peter Drucker's *The Practice of Management*.[4]

Management by objectives had its day as the supposed cure-all of most of the prevailing ills of organizational functioning, much the same way as total quality management (TQM) or continuous quality improvement is emerging as the organizational cure-all of the 1990s. It is interesting to note that the two main reasons why MBO failed to work in many organizations that tried it are the same reasons why TQM is failing in some of its applications:

- absence of sincere top management involvement and commitment
- a focus on the mechanics or implementation of a process rather than on the concept or philosophy behind the process

In many organizations MBO has been utilized as the joint target setting mechanism applied to certain levels of employees. This recognizes that setting and pursuing objectives aimed toward the improvement of performance is beneficial for certain employees, and that managers and certain others are appropriately evaluated, at least in part, on how well they deal with the planning processes involved in developing and pursuing objectives. As important as this aspect of performance can be, however, the use of joint target-setting approaches, including MBO, can do severe damage to fundamental performance appraisal if they are not properly applied.

A SUPPLEMENT, NOT A REPLACEMENT

The problem arising between performance appraisal and joint target setting arises when the latter is applied in such a way as to take over the basic functions of appraisal. Joint target setting can never completely replace performance appraisal, even an appraisal system that is totally and properly job-description based. When joint target setting is allowed the upper hand, the fundamentals of performance appraisal are subverted.

Recall the contention that joint target setting is not properly applied as a remedial process. It applies only when employee performance is at standard or better relative to job description requirements. The employee who is performing below standard may be given some apparent goals, targets, or objectives for improvement, but these are dictated targets—dictated by basic job description requirements and reinforced by the manager. Yet when the manager nudges the employee toward certain objectives because the manager is not satisfied with employee performance, or when the employee suggests certain targets out of knowledge of the manager's dissatisfaction with performance in a specific area, target setting is being used in a remedial sense and is thus usurping a primary role of appraisal.

Even more troublesome is what happens to the requirement for standard performance when joint target setting takes over from performance appraisal. Each and every target developed and pursued supposedly represents improvement over past performance. Each time the employee cycles through the process there are new targets, new objectives. Subsequent targets that involve or overlap parts of the job addressed by earlier targets eventually call for more and more improvement in the same task areas. When the target setting approach is allowed to overshadow fundamental appraisal in this manner, the employee is being evaluated against constantly shifting, steadily growing standards of performance. Each iteration essentially presents a set of new and higher standards, and the employee is eventually caught in a no-win situation because a constant requirement for better than standard has become the standard.

Joint target setting has an important place relative to appraisal, especially for professional, technical, and managerial employees, but it cannot be allowed to absorb the role of performance appraisal. Performance appraisal must be allowed to restrict its focus to the effectiveness with which employees carry out the essential functions of their jobs as defined by their job descriptions.

The concept of a job is an important one. It specifies a person's role, it forms the basis for accepting employment, and it serves as the reference point by which people judge the equity of their treatment. Appraisal systems based in target-setting processes have allowed the target-setting process to regularly redefine the functions that a job will comprise and will therefore subvert the very concept of a job. The integrity of this concept can be restored by focusing appraisal on the continuing functions that define an employee's role.[5]

Goal setting in performance appraisal should in reality be goal setting *with* performance appraisal. Performance appraisal should continue to serve its primary objective of maintaining or improving performance in the job the employee presently holds, while goal setting should concentrate on encouraging accomplishment and innovation while the employee continues to perform at standard or better.

NOTES

1. Len Sandler, "Two-Sided Performance Reviews," *Personnel Journal*, vol. 69, no. 1 (January 1990) p. 76.
2. *Ibid*, p. 77.
3. Jeffrey S. Kane and Kimberly A. Freeman, "MBO and Performance Appraisal: A Mixture That's Not a Solution, Part 1," *Personnel*, vol. 63, no. 12 (December 1986) p. 26.
4. Peter F. Drucker, "Management by Objectives and Self-Control," *The Practice of Management*, (New York: Harper and Row, Publishers, 1954).
5. Jeffrey S. Kane and Kimberly A. Freeman, "MBO and Performance Appraisal: A Mixture That's Not a Solution, Part 2," *Personnel*, vol. 64, no. 2 (February 1987) p. 32.

16

Evaluating Managers
and Professionals

DIFFERING APPRAISAL APPROACHES FOR DIFFERENT EMPLOYEES

No management of an organization that uses a wide variety of employee skills should feel compelled to use a single appraisal approach for all employees. However, many organizations persist in taking a one-size-fits-all approach to appraisal.[1]

When all employees are evaluated using a single mechanism it is bound to be overpowering for some employees and insufficient for others. Yet many health institutions continue to use the same form, the same ground rules, and thus the same general approach for all employees from the unskilled laborer through the highly skilled professional to the manager. In some health care organizations, however, attempts have been made to recognize valid differences in appraisal approaches as related to persons in varying job grades. A few organizations use:

- a two-system approach, evaluating nonexempt employees and exempt employees with different methods
- a two-level approach that distinguishes between managerial employees and nonmanagerial employees
- a three-system approach consisting of one set of rules for nonmanagers, one for managers, and one specific to nursing personnel

It is suggested that the division of appraisal approaches between exempt and nonexempt employees is highly appropriate for most health organizations. One system can apply to the evaluation of unskilled, semiskilled, clerical, and lower level technical employees, while a separate appraisal system can be used for higher level technical employees and for professionals and managers. This latter system will tend to subdivide itself as evaluation criteria are developed and refined and the largest user of criteria-based evaluation—the department of nursing—develops its own specific way of applying the system.

This chapter treats managers and professionals jointly because they are similar in a number of ways. Indeed, a significant proportion of managers in health care are health professionals as well. When compared with the nonexempt work force, managers and professionals and higher level technical employees generally:

- work in positions requiring greater amounts of formal education
- experience more variability in their work and are likely to face a greater number of different problems and challenges
- work within job descriptions that are less precise and more open to interpretation
- have more control over process; that is, within established limits can do the same things in different ways as long as the appropriate results are produced
- regularly exercise individual discretion and judgment in the performance of work

Goal Setting for Managers and Professionals

Goal-setting activities, whether informal joint target-setting exercises or more formal management by objectives programs, can be a helpful and productive part of the appraisal process for professionals, managers, and higher level technical employees (see Chapter 15). However, the precautions of Chapter 15 are in order—goal setting must supplement appraisal and not attempt to replace it. Properly treated as an improvement mechanism, but not as a remedial process, goal setting can help expand an employee's capabilities such that the results are eventually experienced as improved job performance over and above the satisfactory performance identified earlier through performance appraisal.

For the manager, professional, or higher level technical employee, goal setting presents an ideal opportunity for employee participation coupled with employee development.

Self-Appraisal for Managers and Professionals

As mentioned throughout this book, self-appraisal can be a helpful adjunct to most performance appraisal approaches. As also noted elsewhere, however, self-appraisal is best left available as an option to the employee. As far as managerial and professional employees are concerned, it is frequently possible to sell such employees on the value of self-appraisal through a discussion of the merits of the process. Self-appraisal:

- involves the employee more intimately in the appraisal process, taking advantage of the fact that nobody knows the true inner working details of a particular job better than the person who does it every day

- allows the employee to elaborate on aspects of performance that he or she feels may not be completely visible to the appraiser
- encourages the employee to think more than passingly about aspects of his or her performance, and thus to be better prepared for a performance dialogue
- encourages the employee to open up to advance consideration of possible criticism, inevitably reducing the frequency and impact of surprises in appraisal
- provides the employee a view of his or her own performance for comparison with the evaluator's view, potentially highlighting the areas of performance that the parties most need to discuss (For example, if an employee and superior each make evaluations independent of each other on a 15-point list of criteria and later discover their evaluations are similar on all but three points, then the parties know exactly where their subsequent discussion and effort should be focused.)

Still, self-appraisal will not be for everyone. Some will balk at the prospect, fearing that they will be viewed as egotistical if they evaluate themselves higher than the appraiser does, or be seen as lacking self-confidence if they evaluate themselves lower than the appraiser does. And the instant the employee becomes caught up in attempting to second guess the appraiser, most of the potential value of self-appraisal is negated.

Peer Group Appraisal

Peer group appraisal is often applicable to professional or higher level technical employees. It is most potentially valuable for those who work in teams where the success of any single person is largely dependent on the success of the group. As described in Chapter 14, in the discussion of group appraisal methods, the team members evaluate each other as a supplement to—and never a replacement for—individual appraisal of each member by the team's supervisor.

Peer group appraisal will not necessarily apply to all professionals. For those who work essentially alone, or who at least are not ordinarily part of a team or close-knit departmental group, there will be an insufficient peer group for appraisal. Unless there are several peers (there is no fixed magic number, but common sense suggests that at least three or four are necessary) who are intimately familiar with a person's work, preferably to the extent of having their own performance at least partially dependent on that person's efforts, peer group appraisal can be no more than a superficial exercise.

Rarely is peer group appraisal applicable to managers. Some limited input concerning narrow aspects of performance may be possible from other members of a management group, but generally a manager's peers are not in a position to assess a manager's performance in its most important dimensions. Each manager will be focused most of the time on the internal operations of his or her own department; no peers will share this internal view. Evaluation of the manager must remain largely up to the manager's immediate superior.

DIVIDED LOYALTIES: THE PROFESSIONAL AS A SCARCE RESOURCE

In the case of a number of health care occupations two particular sets of circumstances have combined to make certain employees more difficult to manage and have made performance appraisal all the more critical for these employees. Those circumstances are the free agent effect and scarcity.

The free agent concept was well defined by Howard L. Smith and Neill F. Piland. In the organizational sense a free agent is any employee who is unwilling to make a strong commitment to an organization's mission, goals, policies, culture, and strategy for achieving goals.[2] The free agent may be characterized by a primary commitment to an occupation or profession, as opposed to commitment to an organization, and by strong emphasis on interesting and satisfying work experiences, a high degree of self-interest, and a willingness to change organizational affiliations fairly readily.

Scarcity compounds the free agent effect. The so-called free agent who practices an occupation or profession that is in short supply on the employment market automatically acquires more individual clout in dealing with management. When the market for a particular skill becomes a seller's market, two kinds of pressure are possible. Organizations that find themselves short of the scarce skill begin to bid for the services of the practitioners employed elsewhere, creating pressure to increase compensation levels everywhere else as well. And practitioners themselves, sometimes individually, sometimes in concert, use the possibility of higher wages elsewhere to force increased compensation in their present employment.

However, it requires more than just equitable compensation in a particular market area to keep a scarce professional in the organization. Since the scarce professional's primary loyalty may be to the profession, and since this person may place a high premium on interesting and satisfying work experiences, it follows that retention of the scarce professional is more difficult than for many other staff.

Efforts at retention are intended to encourage employees to remain with the organization because they want to remain. There are of course a number of obvious reasons why some employees choose to remain with the organization, among them the economic rewards of salary and employee benefits. Beyond elements of compensation, however, there are less measurable but often more important factors such as:

• recognition and appreciation of work well done
• the opportunity for growth and development
• the expansion of the opportunity for interesting work experiences
• the feeling that one is making a positive contribution

These and other intangible factors are very real needs that employees bring to the job (see the discussion in Chapter 1 of *the basic needs of employees* and *motivators and dissatisfiers*). They are important in employee retention, and properly utilized performance appraisal can help to meet these needs. Appraisal provides recognition and appreciation of work well done, provides for acknowledgment of the employee's contributions, and periodically reinforces these. Coupled with joint target setting, appraisal can set the stage for expanding the employee's opportunity for interesting work experiences, as it is largely the employee's own preferences that determine what the targets will be. This likewise keeps employee development in the forefront; he or she does not simply do the job, but rather continually looks for ways to do the job more efficiently, more effectively, and in a more interesting manner.

Assuming that all other factors are essentially equal or very nearly so, honest, effective performance appraisal can sometimes make the difference between an employee's staying or leaving.

INCREASING IMPORTANCE OF THE APPRAISAL OF MANAGERS

In many organizations it was a long held practice for the managers to evaluate the nonmanagers but to receive no evaluations themselves. This has been changing for quite some time, especially in health care where individual consciousness of the need for appraisal has been increasing steadily.

As more organizations adopt pay-for-performance systems for their managers they encounter an increasing need for managerial appraisal. Such new pay systems demand measures of performance. Level of performance must be assessed to determine level of reward. Since more managers' salary increases or bonuses are being tied directly to performance level there is a growing need for determining performance level in some consistent manner, so monetary reward is related directly to performance appraisal.

Performance appraisal is also becoming more important in supporting termination of a manager when necessary. The termination of a manager for reasons of performance should be supported by reasonably objective documentation indicating that the firing was not arbitrary or capricious. This is especially important in cases involving minority managers or older managers (see Chapter 17).

Performance appraisal is becoming more important as well in support of management development and succession planning. These functions are actually two sides of the same coin. Appraisal supports management development by revealing weaknesses and training needs in present management. Appraisal supports succession planning by suggesting the management skills that should be strengthened and perpetuated through management turnover and by identifying the changes that should be worked into the organization's management capabilities as the organization moves into the future.

Overall, appraisal of the manager is as important as appraisal of the rank-and-file employee if only for one basic reason: the manager is a person with individual needs just as the rank-and-file employee is a person with individual needs.

SUBORDINATE EVALUATION OF THE BOSS

In a 1988 study a number of managers were asked, "If your subordinates were to evaluate your performance, how valuable would you find such feedback for your own personal development?" Three-quarters of those asked said they would find such feedback definitely or extremely valuable.[3] One might wonder if in actual practice the proportion of managers favoring subordinate evaluation would remain as high as three-quarters after they had all experienced subordinate evaluation. However, there are some definite advantages to having subordinate input in the evaluation of the manager. Specifically:

- The rank-and-file employee is often sufficiently close to the manager to see the manager's true work performance.
- The employee is able to see aspects of the manager's conduct that higher management never gets to see.
- The employee is in the best position to judge whether the manager is appropriately visible to the department and available to the employees.
- Because of the rank-and-file employee's unique view of the manager, the employee is able to add perspective to manager development by helping to highlight management training needs that might not otherwise be readily uncovered.

But the disadvantages of subordinate evaluation can at times be significant. There are straightforward personality differences; like everyone else, the individual employee will like some people more or less than others and this will influence the assessment of any particular manager. There are often differences related to age—the older employee may resent the younger boss and rate accordingly; differences related to length of service or experience—the "older" resents the "newer" and rates accordingly; and differences founded in beliefs about capabilities—as, "I know that I could do that job better."

The manager who opts for subordinate evaluation needs to have developed a fairly thick skin. Overall the employees will be relatively kind in their assessments, and in many instances they will, on average, rate managers higher than the managers rate themselves. However, there will be some occasional surprises and some barbs from directions that never occurred to the manager. There also will be some predictable inconsistencies between managers' ratings and employees' ratings of the managers; for example, the overwhelming majority of managers rate themselves higher in the communications skills than their employees rate them.

Because of the shortcomings described above, it is hazardous to use subordinate appraisal to provide specifics about managerial behavior to the appraisal process. However, subordinate evaluations can be helpful in revealing trends and tendencies in a manager's behavior. In other words, if it is something said by just a person or two it is probably not valid, but if nearly everyone raises the same point there is probably something of substance to it.

INDICATORS OF MANAGERIAL PERFORMANCE

The difficulties inherent in establishing objectives and measurements for managers and professionals are frequently underestimated, especially in large, complex organizations.[4] Measurements are especially difficult to establish for both managers and professionals, but for both we can—and always should—begin with up-to-date, comprehensive job descriptions. From these we proceed to develop evaluation criteria: job requirements concisely expressed as actions that should be taken. Specific to managers, there should be four dimensions of managerial performance spelled out in the appraisal. Also contained (probably in multiple places) in every appropriate managerial job description, these four major dimensions of performance are:

- financial management
- productivity
- quality of service
- human resource management

Most managers can be appraised successfully using the above four major indicators of managerial performance.

Financial Management

By far most managers have budget responsibility. An occasional first-line supervisor may not have budget responsibility—perhaps a small-group supervisor in a larger unit, or a lead worker who supervises and works with one or two others, or some such individual who manages the work of a few but answers to a manager who has the budget responsibility. Mostly, however, those who can be called managers usually have responsibility for some aspect of financial management.

In some organizations the annual budget is still prepared "upstairs" and handed down for the managers to work to and live with. It is unfortunate that this practice prevails in some places. A budget is a plan—a financial plan covering a certain period of time—and handing a fully prepared budget down for implementation is expecting the manager to buy into a plan and implement it without having had a voice in its preparation. Ideally, the manager charged with operating to a budget has had a major role in developing that budget.

Whether a particular manager's financial management responsibility is narrowly or broadly defined, that responsibility should be spelled out in the job description and the manager should be evaluated on how well that responsibility is fulfilled. Each clearly definable element of financial management is a potential appraisal criterion. The budget-related criteria on which a department manager may be evaluated might include, for example:

- how well the manager is able to keep overall expenditures under control relative to the budget; that is, how close to the budget target the actual expenditures fall
- how well the manager is able to balance and control the separate major elements of the budget—personnel costs and nonlabor expenses
- how closely the use of overtime is monitored and controlled
- how closely the use of temporary help is monitored and controlled
- how well any other particular element of departmental expense is monitored and controlled relative to spending targets
- how effectively the manager is able to reallocate resources to continue meeting overall budget targets when certain expenditures increase beyond the manager's reasonable ability to control them

The foregoing financial management criteria, and others that may be appropriate to individual managers' situations, lend themselves to measurement fairly well. For example, the manager might have an overall target of finishing the year with results that are within 2 percent of budget, or perhaps a specific target specifying that the department's overtime budget cannot be exceeded or that overtime and temporary help combined cannot exceed budget but that resources may be reallocated from one to the other depending on need.

The most effective measures will be those that the manager and the manager's superior or appraiser agree on in advance as reasonable. If these measures represent attainable goals, the manager should be willing to buy in to them. In later appraising the manager and assessing relative success, it remains for the superior to determine whether certain occurrences that caused unexpected expenditures were within the manager's control, and if they were not totally within the manager's control, what the manager could have done to compensate at least partially for the undesired financial effects.

Any manager who has budget responsibility—and this includes the vast majority of even the lowest level managers—can be evaluated on financial management with a considerable degree of objectivity.

Productivity

Depending on function, most managers can be evaluated on some aspect of department productivity. Much of productivity measurement requires some form of counting of departmental output. Admittedly it can be costly and time consuming to provide full scale productivity standards where none at all exist, but it is often possible to come up with overall indicators or guidelines that can be applied. The productivity measures that might apply in various managers' departments include:

- number of patients served
- number of items processed (for example, the number of bills produced by a billing section; the number of work orders completed by a maintenance crew; etc.)
- the number of cases or visits handled
- the number of procedures completed (for example, laboratory tests or radiology procedures)

As with financial management, the opportunity for objective measurement of productivity in appraisal is present. However, the practicality of objective measurement will vary considerably depending on what may or may not already be in place. A department that has a productivity monitoring system in place and operating has everything the evaluator needs to readily appraise the manager's departmental productivity with objective measures. If no such standards exist it is suggested that the appraiser research some potential guidelines for overall operation of the manager's function and proceed to negotiate some productivity targets with the manager. With a little advance planning it is possible to be able to evaluate most managers' productivity objectively, if perhaps somewhat crudely.

Quality of Service

It is also possible to appraise many managers fairly objectively on the quality of work produced by their departments. These managers should, of course, also be appraising their employees on work quality. Again depending on function, quality is at least as objectively measurable as productivity. Productivity statistics often include quality information or data that can be converted readily to quality information. Direct measures of quality might include:

- error rate for any activity (typing, data entry, billing, etc.)
- rate or percentage of procedures repeated (as in tests repeated in a laboratory or films retaken in radiology)
- percentage or amount of downtime (unproductive time)
- number of citations, violations, or discrepancies upon inspection or survey
- success (or failure) rate for virtually any procedure or activity

As with productivity, the department that has a monitoring system in place has a running start on the provision of quality standards for managerial performance appraisal. Also as with productivity, where specific standards are lacking it is possible to begin with some estimated, mutually agreed-on quality indicators that the manager can work toward.

Human Resource Management

This is by far the least quantifiable of the four areas of management performance discussed here, and it is often the most important area of management performance. Like the three previously discussed dimensions of performance, its emphasis can vary dramatically from manager to manager. Generally, however, the greater the manager's number of direct reporting employees, the greater the manager's human resource management responsibility.

This is one major performance area for which the appraiser's judgments will remain largely qualitative or subjective. It is hardly fair and certainly not practical to try to "count the complaints" about a specific manager or arising from a specific department and judge the manager on that basis. However, the appraiser should be alert to the kinds of information that say something of substance about a manager's human resource management or human relations performance. These kinds of information are such that quick assessments should not be made. Rather, except for glaring breaches of policy or protocol by a manager, assessments of a manager's performance in this area should accrue from the emergence of clear trends or tendencies the appraiser can address confidently in dealing with the manager.

The relative acceptability of a manager's human relations performance can be inferred from a number of kinds of information, including:

- how well employee complaints appear to be resolved within the department. If employees are chronically going up the chain of command or accessing formal processes to get their complaints heard, they might be encountering rigidity within the department.
- how well the manager follows disciplinary practices. Does the manager frequently attempt to fire prematurely or without complete backup documentation? Do disciplinary processes seem to be applied inconsistently? Does this department seem to generate dramatically more or fewer disciplinary actions than might be expected?
- how well the manager follows personnel procedures in interviewing job candidates and hiring new employees, and the apparent frequency of complaints or problems concerning hiring processes.
- the rate or frequency with which the manager's department seems to attract employment related complaints and legal actions from attorneys and advocacy agencies (state human rights agencies, the Equal Employment Opportunity Commission, etc.).
- trends and tendencies as revealed through exit interviews. Rarely is it wise or even marginally justified to allow a manager's appraisal to be swayed one way or another by the comments on one or two exit interviews. However, similarity of comments accruing over a significant period of time can tell the appraiser much about the manager's style. For example, if two-thirds of the exit interviews from a given department suggest the presence of morale problems, there are probably morale problems in that group. And if most exits describe the manager as fair and understanding, that is probably true as well.
- how well the manager applies internal procedures and observes higher management's requirements. (Consider, for example, how well the manager observes performance appraisal requirements. Managers should be measured on how well they handle the performance appraisal process. This builds in accountability and demonstrates that the appraisal process is valued by the organization.[5])

This list could be made considerably longer, but the point has been established. Anything that is indicative of management style and approach and basic treatment of people over time is a legitimate indicator of a manager's human resource management performance. It falls to the appraiser to learn about the subordinate manager's performance in sufficient depth to be able to render the necessary judgments.

A BALANCING ACT

Most managers' evaluations will necessarily be a blend of considerations of financial management, productivity, quality, and human resource management. The manager with few employees but with a large, complex budget may be evaluated more on financial management than on the other factors; a manager with many employees working in critical patient care functions may be evaluated largely on quality and human relations; a supervisor in charge of a maintenance crew may be evaluated largely on productivity and quality and barely at all on financial management.

Also, the person evaluating the manager must recognize that most of the factors discussed above are interrelated most of the time, and that none of them—especially the first three, financial management, productivity, and quality of service—can be treated in total isolation from the others. It is possible, for example, to make productivity look very good by committing extra resources to the job—but doing so will be at the expense of exceeding the budget. The interrelationships between and among cost, quality, and output are complex and varied, and any one of these that is appraised must always be considered in the light of the others.

NOTES

1. Charles R. McConnell, *Managing the Health Care Professional,* (Gaithersburg, MD: Aspen Publishers, Inc., 1984) p. 106.
2. Howard L. Smith and Neill F. Piland, "Managing Free Agents in Health Care Organizations: A Supervisory Challenge," *The Health Care Supervisor,* vol. 8, no. 3 (April 1990) p. 54.
3. Glenn M. McEvoy, "Evaluating the Boss," *Personnel Administrator,* vol. 33, no. 9 (September 1988) p. 118.
4. Robert J. Sahl, "Design Effective Performance Appraisals," *Personnel Journal,* vol. 69, no. 10 (October 1990) p. 53.
5. Marjorie G. Derven, "The Paradox of Performance Appraisals," *Personnel Journal,* vol. 69, no. 2 (February 1990) p. 111.

17
Legal Implications
of Appraisal

THE LEGAL MINEFIELD OF APPRAISAL

Performance appraisal presents a steadily growing number of potential legal traps for the unwary evaluator.

Wrongful Discharge

Many wrongful termination lawsuits are an outgrowth of inadequate performance appraisal procedures. A 1988 study concluded that employees were at that time three times more likely to sue their employers than they were in 1980.[1] Given this combination of facts and circumstances, plus plenty of evidence to suggest that lawsuits by disgruntled former employees continue to increase in frequency, we can conclude that performance appraisal has some considerable legal implications that probably will be with us for a very long time.

Wrongful discharge complaints have indeed been on the increase for several years, and performance appraisals are invariably key elements in these complaints. In many states—perhaps 30 or more—personnel policy manuals and employee handbooks have been found in the courts to be forms of employment contracts. These "contracts" generally promise, either directly or by implication, continued employment for "good performance." If a discharged employee's appraisals indicate essentially good performance, the stage is set for a wrongful discharge complaint.

Laws and Performance Appraisal

Most legal complaints about performance appraisal have involved violations of rights directly provided by Title VII of the Civil Rights Act of 1964.[2] That is, up to late 1991 they involved violations of the Civil Rights Act of 1964. Since late 1991 the activity understandably has been shifting to the Civil Rights Act of

1991, with its expanded provisions for jury trials, enhanced awards, and harsher penalties.

However, performance appraisals can figure prominently in actions initiated under several other laws, including:

- Executive Orders 11246 (1965) and 11375 (1967), forbidding discrimination on the basis of race, color, religion, sex, or national origin in the employment practices of federal agencies and departments.
- The Rehabilitation Act (1973 and 1974), prohibiting discrimination on the basis of handicap in federally funded programs.
- The Pregnancy Discrimination Act (1978), amending Title VII so that discrimination in employment on the basis of pregnancy is prohibited.
- The Equal Pay Act (1963), prohibiting sex-based differences in pay for work that is essentially equal.
- The Age Discrimination in Employment Act (1967, 1978, and 1986), prohibiting employers from discriminating on the basis of age, and prohibiting mandatory retirement for most employees.

Special Concerns About Age Discrimination

Performance appraisal evidence appears to have considerable relevance in complaints filed under the Age Discrimination in Employment Act (ADEA). The three most common forms of personnel actions giving rise to ADEA complaints are: promotions, retirements or layoffs, and discharges.[3]

Promotion decisions require that the employer show only that the complaining employee was not as qualified as the candidate selected for an expanded role in the organization.[4] Honest, accurate, complete performance appraisals for all parties concerned can determine the outcomes of such complaints.

A layoff or retirement requires the employer to demonstrate that the laid-off or retired employee was not as qualified as those selected to remain.[5] As with promotional decisions, performance appraisal information can play a significant role in complaint resolution.

Note that complaints involving the issues of promotion and layoff or retirement usually do not turn on whether an individual was performing at a so-called satisfactory level or to some specific standard. Rather, in these actions the assessment of performance is relative; that is, performance documentation is used to show that one person was or was not performing at a higher or lower level than certain others. In point of fact, all employees named in such a dispute well might have been rated consistently better than satisfactory. However, requirements can be quite different as far as discharge is concerned.

A discharge decision generally will not be upheld if it can be shown that the employee was considered to have been performing at minimally acceptable levels. Therefore, under ADEA, as well as in complaints arising under other laws, discharge for reasons of supposed poor performance is readily challenged if performance appraisals indicate acceptable performance.

WHY HAVE APPRAISAL?

Although employers have no legal obligation initially to establish a formal system for appraising performance, once an employer institutes a system, the employer may have inadvertently established a contract with its employees to use the system for the purpose for which it was established and in the manner in which it was described to employees.[6] If it is indeed true that a performance appraisal system is seen under the law as simply one more form of contract affecting employment, why have a system at all? Why not simply avoid all of the legal risks of performance appraisal by not appraising performance?

The simple answer to the foregoing question is, of course, that in spite of the legal risks appraisal is needed for a number of reasons. First, recall the objectives of performance appraisal as presented early in this volume: to maintain or improve performance in the job the employee presently holds and to assist employee development. These are not simply "nice things to do;" they reflect service to organizational needs and individual needs. For the sake of the organization and the individual, it is desirable to maintain good performance; for the sake of both it is desirable to improve performance where there is room to do so. And employee development is necessary so the organization can keep filling its personnel needs and the capable individual can pursue promotion and growth.

Beyond its role in filling a common-sense management need, appraisal also exists in many health care organizations because various accreditation and regulatory bodies have mandated that it will exist.

Also, as suggested throughout this discussion of appraisal's legal implications, it is the role of performance appraisal to provide a basis for making employment decisions—for deciding on promotions, transfers, layoffs, discharges, and often pay raises. Consider how these decisions would be made were there no consistent appraisal of employee performance. Most likely they would be made the way they were made in the years before appraisal—arbitrarily, based on likes, dislikes, biases, personalities, and whatever a particular decision maker cared to factor into a decision. Appraisal may appear to be risky in a legal sense, but what makes it so are the traps and pitfalls of an imperfect, human-driven process. We can be reasonably assured that the legal entanglements arising from various employment decisions would be far more numerous and considerably more troublesome in the complete absence of performance appraisal.

MINIMIZING POTENTIAL LEGAL PROBLEMS: FOLLOW THE SYSTEM

Focus on Performance

As mentioned early in this book and repeated often, the appraisal process should focus on performance and not on person. It should view the job, not the person who does the job; it should assess performance, never personality; it should deal with the results of behavior, not attempt to identify the causes of behavior. The more an appraisal wanders into the realm of personal traits and subjective judgments, the more vulnerable is that appraisal to legal challenge.

Be Specific and Objective

A performance appraisal is no place for generalities. However, an evaluator who gives no thought to making an appraisal until it is time to start writing has nothing to call on but human memory. Since few if any managers can remember everything pertinent to every employee, it is common to find generalizations arising from the few things the manager can indeed remember.

Generalizations rarely survive legal scrutiny. Therefore, it is usually necessary for the manager to gather information on each employee throughout the appraisal period. Anecdotal note files can be extremely helpful, but they should be maintained with care. Maintain notes relating to positive and negative instances of performance and later fold this information into the appraisal, cleaning out the notes once the appraisal is written. Be specific in your notes, always including dates and times and specific occurrences, and keep all notes related strictly to job performance and personnel policy.

Keep all anecdotal notes as objective as possible and keep them completely free from labeling and name calling. Put nothing on paper that you would be ashamed to see made public; all documents, even a manager's most private and informal notes, legally can be demanded by a complainant's attorney once a formal legal action is begun.

Since anecdotal notes can do no harm if they do not exist, periodically purge anecdotal files of outdated and irrelevant material. Once a note is used in an appraisal, or once it is decided that a particular note is not needed for appraisal purposes, get rid of it. Do this regularly with anecdotal notes when there is no legal conflict brewing, but not when legal action has commenced. Destroying related documents once a charge has been filed is itself an illegal act.

Apply the System Consistently

Problems arise with appraisal when an aggrieved party is able to convince others that an appraisal system was not applied consistently from person to person, or that certain individuals or classes of people were treated differently primarily because of who they were.

The best defense against problems of inconsistent application is evaluator training (see Chapter 4). Evaluators require intensive training in how the system is applied, preferably in group settings so that many evaluators receive the same information in the same form. This training must be reinforced periodically, and each evaluator should have the system's instructions in writing for constant reference.

Consistency also must show in the way a particular evaluator appraises his or her employees. Each performance criterion must be assessed in the same way for every employee in the group; there should be no question of bearing down hard on some while going easy on others. The employee who may charge that, "The boss is picking on me," may convince others of this if a marginal or negative appraisal in question consists of much more writing and far more detail than all other appraisals in the department.

Observe All System Steps and Timetables

Usually at the end of the performance appraisal interview the employee is called on to sign his or her appraisal. The evaluator should make every reasonable effort to obtain this signature. However, the evaluator has the responsibility of ensuring that the employee knows what the signature indicates.

The employee's signature should simply acknowledge that he or she has discussed this evaluation and received a copy. Ideally the form should bear a legend at the signature block indicating something on the order of: "Signature acknowledges receipt of this form." It is important for the employee to understand that signing the appraisal does not mean complete acceptance of or agreement with its contents. It is also important, however, to be able to establish that the employee did indeed receive the appraisal.

If an employee refuses to sign an appraisal in spite of all explanations about the meaning of the signature, do not force the issue. Rather, simply note on the form that the employee refused to sign, and date and initial the note.

It is extremely important to make certain that the appropriate copy of every performance appraisal (usually the original) ends up in each employee's personnel file. When called for in a legal proceeding but found missing from the personnel file, it may be readily concluded that a particular appraisal does not exist. Depending on who is looking for a certain appraisal and why, an appraisal located anywhere else but in the personnel file may be considered suspect. In one particular case in which two or three years' worth of appraisals for several people in a department were found in a manager's desk drawer in a state of partial completion—most of the required signatures were lacking—the complainants charged that the appraisals had been fabricated after the legal action began. The charge of fabrication and the incomplete state of the appraisals were enough to greatly diminish the potential value of these documents.

Once in a while it is necessary to alter an employee's appraisal score after it has become a matter of record. Occasionally an error is discovered after the fact, and sometimes an employee protests a score with sufficiently good information that the evaluator agrees to a change. If a change is made to a score that is already in the official record, the change should be noted in the personnel file and both parties—employee and evaluator—should initial and date the change. Once an appraisal score is part of a permanent record—and this is generally interpreted to mean once the score is discussed with the employee—it should never be altered without the employee's knowledge.

"SEE YOU IN COURT"

Most Title VII, ADEA, and other complaints that eventually go to court usually do so only after a considerable period of time following the incidents that sparked the complaints. It is in fact sometimes several years between the original complaint and the subsequent court proceeding.

Memories fade over the intervening years. The perspectives and perceptions of the parties, already differing at the start to a degree capable of fostering the complaint, become distorted and often grow farther apart. Often the best evidence of what happened and of who said what about whom is in the performance appraisal records. Or it *should* be the best evidence.

The role that the official record plays in a legal proceeding cannot be stressed too strongly. In the overwhelming percentage of cases there is strong reliance on the contents of the record. If an individual was discharged for substandard or marginal performance but the person's personnel record contains nothing but standard or acceptable evaluations, performance will be considered to have been satisfactory.

The reliance on the personnel record is often total or very nearly so. If something is in the file as part of the official record, it is generally taken as factual. If some action, occurrence, or result claimed by either party is not part of the record, more often than not it is treated as though it never happened.

Once in the courtroom, all dimensions of the performance appraisal become important. Any deviation from the established appraisal system—scores given without comments, comments without scores, signatures missing, dates missing, forms partially completed in other ways, evaluation deadlines missed, inappropriate remarks entered, entire appraisals missing—is an invitation to legal challenge and an opportunity for a plaintiff's attorney to make an accusation or create an area of doubt.

Jury trials, which have been made more readily available by the Civil Rights Act of 1991, are especially hazardous. The well-known legal standard of criminal proceedings, beyond a reasonable doubt, does not apply in civil proceedings (lawsuits). Rather, the jury in a civil proceeding is urged to decide more along the lines of whether it is more likely that a particular act did or did not take place. Thus the standard of proof in a civil proceeding is not nearly as rigid as in a criminal case.

Also, juries consist largely of working people who tend to extend the benefit of the doubt to the individual over the organization. Often there is not an outcome as clear as yes or no or guilty or not guilty. Rather, unless there is a single, clearly stated charge filed under one particular law (often the charges cite multiple violations of various laws, all surrounding the central issue), the results may be split although tending strongly in one direction or the other.

THE BIGGEST TRAP

A major problem leading to difficulties with internal disciplinary procedures and with the external legal system is presented by lenient appraisals. Time and again, evaluators who give marginal or substandard performers satisfactory appraisals will later try to discharge an employee, deny a promotion, or initiate some other personnel action because of performance. Regardless of what the evaluator may think about an individual's performance, it is what the evaluator commits to paper that ordinarily will prevail. In making an appraisal that calls the person satisfactory, the appraiser is stating officially that the employee is doing good, competent work. The appraiser is saying that the employee's work is acceptable.

Many organizations have been put at risk by their own managers, who exaggerate employee performance levels. When it becomes necessary to weed out marginal performers during business downturns or other periods of financial hardship, trouble arises because the marginal performers are all satisfactory on paper.

Every evaluator is urged to be honest regarding performance, yet to be generous concerning interpretations of what is considered standard or satisfactory. Do not be lenient to the point of covering up true substandard performance, but neither be so rigid as to expect near perfection as the standard. Satisfactory is not perfection; there should remain plenty of room to improve over that level. However, satisfactory is acceptable.

As an appraiser, never render an evaluation that you honestly do not believe. However, when you deliver an honest substandard appraisal you need to back up your assessment with performance measurements or other specific information. If you are not prepared with specifics, you are not ready to give the appraisal.

If pay increases are somehow linked to performance or are in any way discretionary with the manager, never recommend a pay increase for a marginal performer if you are doing it simply to be kind or to avoid making waves. It is far better to face the difficult evaluation in the present than to fight an unjust discharge or age discrimination charge later. Similar to a satisfactory appraisal in the personnel file, a raise in pay is considered evidence that the employee has been performing acceptably.

Legal Appraisals from Legal Job Descriptions

In various employment-related legal actions, job descriptions come under as much scrutiny as performance appraisals, and sometimes more. Since much is made of the necessity to stress performance and focus on the person's results in doing the job, it follows that the safest and most useful evaluation criteria arise from elements of the job itself.

Clear, clean criteria for performance appraisal come from clear, properly written job descriptions. It should be clear by now to most evaluators that performance criteria should all arise from the requirements of the job. It should follow that the legally safest performance appraisals arise from properly written job descriptions. None of the elements of this interrelationship of systems and subsystems—neither position analysis, job description, job standard, performance appraisal, nor whatever else leads into or away from these—exists in a vacuum.

ETHICAL EMPHASIS

Appraisal of the performance, and not of the person, is much more than a simple caveat of performance appraisal. Consider the following:

> Workplace ethics require that people be judged *solely* on the basis of job performance. Ethics requires managers to eliminate such things as favoritism, friendship, sex bias, race bias, or age bias from promotion and pay decisions (it is, of course, also *unlawful* to take sex, race, or age into account).[7]

The foregoing appeared in a report that identified ethics as a bottom-line issue in today's work organizations. In giving voice and weight to this fundamental belief—*Workplace ethics require that people be judged solely on the basis of job performance*—we arrive at the best business reason of all for assessing the performance and not the person: to do otherwise is unethical. What the person is should matter not at all; what the person does should count for everything.

THE LEGALLY CRUCIAL ELEMENTS OF APPRAISAL

How performance appraisal has fared in the legal system through a significant number of cases permits some reasonable conclusions as to the characteristics of a legally defensible appraisal system. Some of these characteristics were alluded to in Chapter 4 and all are embodied within the characteristics presented in Chapter 13.

The crucial elements of a legally defensible performance appraisal system are:

1. *The system is based on the job, with the appraisal criteria arising from an analysis of the legitimate requirements of the position.* This is, again, the embodiment of the oft-repeated admonition to focus on the job itself and not on the person who does the job.
2. *Performance is assessed using objective criteria as much as possible given the unique requirements of the job.* That is, there must be reasons behind the assessments rendered, reasons that amount to more than simply the unsupported subjective opinion of the appraiser.
3. *The appraisers have been trained in the use of the system and possess written instructions on how the appraisal is to be completed.* This establishes that any appraiser is as reasonably capable of evaluating performance as any other appraiser using the same system, and that the system can be expected to be applied as intended.
4. *The results of each appraisal are reviewed and discussed with the employee.* This is a key area of concern. Documentation of performance problems and efforts to correct them are necessary if an employee fails to improve and must be let go, but it is also necessary to establish that the employee knew about the difficulties. Thus the legally defensible appraisal system can be used to demonstrate that the employee knew of the problems and was given the opportunity to correct them.

NOTES

1. Patricia S. Eyres, "Legally Defensible Performance Appraisal Systems," *Personnel Journal*, vol. 68, no. 7 (July 1989) p. 58.

2. Shelley R. Burchett and Kenneth P. DeMeuse, "Performance Appraisal and the Law," *Personnel*, vol. 62, no. 7 (July 1985) p. 33.

3. Michael H. Schuster and Christopher S. Miller, "Performance Appraisal and the Age Discrimination in Employment Act," *Personnel Administrator,* vol. 29, no. 3, p. 48.

4. *Ibid*, p. 57.

5. *Ibid*.

6. Roberta V. Romberg, "Performance Appraisal, 1: Risks and Rewards," *Personnel*, vol. 63, no. 8 (August 1986) p. 21.

7. Commerce Clearing House, "1991 SHRM/CCH Survey," *Human Resources Management (*June 26, 1991) p. 1.

18

Making the Best of a
Less-Than-Ideal System

THE CRITICAL ELEMENT IN APPRAISAL

Regardless of the shape of a given appraisal system or the state of its administration at any time, the critical element in the system's operation remains the human element. Honestly and conscientiously applied by people who fully believe in the value of performance appraisal, even a flawed system can produce more usable results than a supposedly ideal system that is not as honestly and conscientiously applied.

Faced with the need to accomplish performance appraisal with a system that is clearly inadequate, you can choose to run through the process superficially, staying as uninvolved personally as possible, and crank out a document that looks like a performance appraisal. You can then use this document as the reason to hold a one-on-one discussion that may call itself an appraisal interview but that somehow fails to address appraisal's true objectives in any meaningful way. Having done so will probably allow you to say—if not actually believe—that you have fulfilled the performance appraisal dimension of your management responsibilities.

On the other hand, faced with the need to accomplish performance appraisal with a system that is inadequate, you can try to make as much sense of the process as possible, applying the parts that are usable and de-emphasizing the rest. As an individual manager responsible for appraising your own employees' performance, you can ensure that fair appraisal occurs within the limits of your department regardless of the system used by the organization as a whole.

MAKE IT LEGALLY DEFENSIBLE

Recall from the preceding chapter the four crucial elements of a legally defensible performance appraisal system:

1. The system is based on the job, with the appraisal criteria arising from an analysis of the legitimate requirements of the position.

2. Performance is assessed using objective criteria as much as possible given the unique requirements of the job.
3. The appraisers have been trained in the use of the system and possess written instructions on how the appraisal is completed.
4. The results of each appraisal are reviewed and discussed with the employee.

To make the best of an inadequate system one must try initially to build in legal defensibility where it may be lacking because of the system's requirements.

Job-Based Appraisals

The first two of the four legally crucial elements of appraisal can be addressed simultaneously. A complete lack of connection to the specific job will not be a concern with most present systems because of the visibly growing emphasis in health care on criteria-based appraisal. However, one may encounter the occasional system in which job requirements and personality traits are mixed, or, in the extreme, one might face an old-style personality based appraisal approach that embodies a list of criteria like those of Table 18–1. In this extreme case, to approach legal defensibility it is up to the individual manager to replace or support certain items of the inappropriate criteria with job-based criteria and, where possible, establish a degree of objectivity in their assessment.

When preparing to appraise a particular employee, lay out that person's job description alongside the so-called appraisal criteria. (If there is no job description you will first have to create one.) Then look for the relationships between the legitimate requirements of the position and the appraisal system's evaluation points, and for your own departmental purposes rewrite as many of the system's criteria as possible in terms of the position's requirements. Some examples follow.

Table 18–1 Inadequate Appraisal "Criteria"

1. Quality of Work	7. Dependability
2. Volume of Work	8. Attitude
3. Effectiveness	9. Cooperativeness
4. Job Knowledge	10. Interpersonal Relations
5. Adaptability	11. Attendance
6. Initiative	12. Appearance

- For a phlebotomist, "quantity of work" might be replaced in part with "Complete routine morning specimen collection rounds by 9:00 A.M. daily." Further, establish what constitutes satisfactory performance with a criterion like: "Standard = completion by 9:00 A.M. at least four days out of five."
- For a staff nurse, "quality of work" might be replaced in part with "Maintain thorough and accurate nurses' notes for each patient chart," accompanied by an associated standard indicating the error percentage, or perhaps number of omissions per time period, that constitutes standard performance.
- For a preventive maintenance mechanic, "initiative" might be replaced in part with "Make minor repairs as problems are discovered in the normal course of work, and report unusual circumstances that bear investigation and may require possibly extensive repairs." The associated standard for this item may be a simple statement as to whether the person does or does not do as required (but if does not is ever the appraiser's determination, the appraiser needs to cite specific examples of how this mechanic apparently failed to address an unforeseen situation).
- For a considerable number of employees, certainly including most managers, professionals, and technical personnel, "dependability" might be replaced with a criterion like "Meets assignment deadlines most of the time. Keeps manager notified of potential delays and schedule changes. Is generally prompt, punctual, and responsive." Some subjectivity is certainly embodied in assesssing someone under these requirements (How immediate is "prompt"?), but if acceptable a person can be positively assessed in a few words and if generally unacceptable, once again some specifics can be provided (missed deadlines, etc.).
- "Attendance" can be assessed for almost any employee. But the key in assessing attendance lies not in simply labeling it as good, poor, or whatever. Rather, it needs to be assessed against a standard of performance that may be as specific as spelling out a range of days missed in a year that constitutes unacceptable attendance.

In the foregoing manner it is possible to more or less force fit job-based criteria and assessments into an older, inappropriate personality based criteria set. With a bit of creativity and effort it is possible to translate most job descriptions into enough job-based criteria to legitimately assess perhaps eight or nine of the dozen characteristics listed in Table 18-1. Depending on whether the appraiser is required to turn in scores for all characteristics, unused characteristics can either be left blank or given the average score of all assessed characteristics.

This process can involve a great deal of work for the appraising manager, especially if most of the department's employees have unique job descriptions. However, the most time-consuming part of the work—developing all of the necessary evaluation criteria from the job descriptions and fitting them to the corresponding characteristics—need be done only once, thereafter to be altered only as job descriptions change. In following this process the individual appraiser can replace subjective personality judgments with more objective assessments of job performance, thus improving the system's legal defensibility several times over.

Appraiser Training and Instruction

If periodic training in the organization's performance appraisal system is available, the appraiser should take advantage of this. If the system is old and ill-suited to today's requirements, there may be no formal training as such even offered. However, the individual manager with a desire to learn about performance appraisal usually can acquire some instruction, if even one-on-one, from someone responsible for administering the system (usually someone in the human resource department) or from another manager experienced in performance appraisal.

Whether the appraiser participates in one-on-one instruction, in-house training classes, or perhaps outside seminars or workshops concerning performance appraisal, a fairly detailed record of the training should be kept.

Perhaps even more important than establishing that there has been training is showing that the appraiser has access to written instructions concerning how to apply the system. These instructions usually exist somewhere in the organization—again, human resources would be the place to begin looking—although, if the system is old and weak and system administration is lax, few may be aware of the existence of instructions.

Get the instructions and learn them. If they are inadequate as they stand, modify them to suit your needs. If no appraisal instructions at all can be found within the organization, write out your own. Thoroughly document the way you make performance appraisals and be prepared to demonstrate that you apply this same process to each appraisal for each employee.

This activity may not accomplish much in terms of making the organization's appraisal system more legally defensible; if the system as a whole is indefensible, no amount of instruction in its use will change that. However, it is likely that your specific appraisal approach will ensure that the appraisals you produce for your own employees are generally more acceptable than what the system produces in other hands.

The Appraisal Interview

The requirement that the results of each appraisal be reviewed and discussed with the employee gives the appraiser the greatest measure of control over whether appraisal is to succeed or fail within the organization. The manager sees everything that goes into an appraisal: all of the information gathering, the creation of criteria, the writing, the discussion, and so on. However, to most employees not much of the process is visible other than the discussion, that is, the appraisal interview. To the average employee, the performance appraisal discussion is the appraisal, my evaluation, or my review. Except for the employee copy of the appraisal form there may be no other part of the entire appraisal process visible to the employee. The interview is certainly the most important part of the process to the employee.

The appraiser can get positive mileage out of even a weak system by making certain that an honest, open appraisal conference takes place—and that it takes place on time. At this conference the employee needs to hear about what is right and how it is appreciated and what is wrong and how it ought to be corrected. The appraisal interview also promotes legal defensibility by serving as the forum in which the employee learns of perceived performance problems, if any, and further learns what must be done to correct those problems.

NO SIMPLE SOLUTIONS

If you find it necessary, perhaps as a basic organizational requirement placed on all managers, to utilize a performance appraisal system that is less than appropriate to today's employee circumstances and external legal and regulatory requirements, the following steps may be helpful:

- Stress the positive elements of the system while playing down (or ignoring, if possible) the less desirable or potentially legally troublesome elements of the system.
- Adhere strictly to an updated job description in selecting performance criteria for assessment.
- Try whenever possible to inject some objectivity into the assessment of the normally subjective.
- Be rigorously consistent in applying the system from employee to employee.
- Make every effort to keep personal likes and dislikes completely out of the process.
- Always thoroughly discuss performance with the employee.
- Make your objections to the existing system known to higher management and to the human resource department, along with your suggestions for correction and improvement.

STRENGTHENING THE EMPLOYEE-MANAGER RELATIONSHIP

The essence of performance appraisal is interpersonal communication.

If managers think about communicating first, they will plan for the performance with the employee and clarify, together, their understanding of expectations and standards—all before performance begins.[1]

Performance appraisal and communication in the employee-manager relationship are strongly mutually supportive. A strong, open, honest relationship between employee and manager enhances open, honest, and constructive appraisal; open, honest, constructive performance appraisal strengthens the relationship between employee and manager.

As set forth in the preface, and reiterated here, over and above appraisal itself the most important element in assessing performance is the relationship that exists between manager and employee. *If the relationship between manager and employee is all that it should be, then appraisal will be a mere formality because both parties will know where they stand with each other at all times.*

NOTE

1. Roger J. Plachy, "Appraisal Scales That Measure Performance Outcomes and Job Results," *Personnel*, vol. 60, no. 3 (May-June 1983) p. 57.

Index